97 Speaks

LESSONS *from the* DECADES

Babette Hughes

97 Speaks: Lessons from the Decades
© 2020 by Babette Hughes

ISBN: 978-0-9979774-8-6

The events described within this compilation are the author's
personal thoughts and recollections. The dialogue is written to
the best of the author's recount of the events that took place.

Certain historical liberties were taken on some pages of this
book.

Book Cover Illustration & Design by Vincent Hughes
Interior Design by Danielle H. Acee

Lamplight Press, Austin, TX

Printed in the United States of America

For Eric and Steve
forever

I am grateful to Shannon Wood,
world-class reader, editor and friend,
for her encouragement and insight.

Unless you die first, you're going to get old.
—Anonymous

Author's note

In Ibsen's *The Doll's House* the final curtain drops abruptly, leaving the playgoers wondering what happened to Nora after she "…slams the door on her husband and takes off into the snow to make her own way in the world." Readers of my memoir, *Lost and Found,* may also have been left to wonder what happened after I left my husband and home… "Now alone, it was as if the future slipped into this house like a phantom, unknown and dangerous and thrilling."

My story is about murder, family, and the search for the authentic self. Beginning in the 1920's when my bootlegging father, Louis Rosen, and his innocent brother-in-law, Adolph Adelson, were killed in Rosen's turf war with the Mafia.

1

Prohibition Lures the Mafia

She was laughed at and feared, a ridiculous figure smashing up bars with her fevered axe, getting arrested and beaten again and again, which did nothing to contain her passion for her mission: to make drinking alcohol illegal. Carrie Nation was born in 1846, as Carrie Amelia Moore, in poverty to a mentally unstable mother. She married a young physician, Charles Floyd, in 1867 whom she soon left because of his alcoholism. In 1877 she married David Nation, a lawyer, who divorced her on the grounds of desertion.

You could draw a line from her birth in 1846 to my father's, forty-four years later in 1895. Both became passionately involved with alcohol, albeit on different sides. And when prohibition became the law of the land in 1920, my father, Lou Rosen, found the career he was born to.

He was the black sheep of the family, the bad boy. He started crap games in the boys' bathroom in the ninth grade. When strikers picketed the family bakery, sixteen-year-old Lou went after them with a baseball bat and killed one of them, for which he was sent to jail briefly as a juvenile. At the striker's funeral ten thousand people lined up on both sides of Woodland Avenue as sixty union members marched four abreast following the casket.

He lifted money from the family's bakery cash register as an adolescent and gambled and cheated on my mother as an adult. A story my Uncle Mike told me with laughter was that when Lou was seen with another woman he, Mike, swore to my mother that it was he, not her husband, who was with the woman. I didn't know what I hated more—the cheating or the laughter. I think it was the laughter.

Lou was one of nine children and step-siblings in Cleveland, Ohio. His parents—my grandparents—had a bakery on 105th Street. The business required hard work—bread and rolls had to be baked in the middle of the night, ovens and counters scrubbed, the preparation of deliveries for a horse and wagon, customers served over the counter from early morning to late in the day. Everyone worked: the older children, the parents, grandparents, a union man looking for day work. Everyone that is except Lou, who would run away, return when he ran out of money, and then repeat the cycle all over again.

Lured by accounts of bootlegging riches, the Mafia came to the U.S. from Sicily with the kind of organized violence unknown in the United States. My father had put together a functioning bootlegging operation as soon as Prohibition became the law of the land in 1920. Two years later, in 1922, a *capo famiglia* or Mafia Boss by the name of Joe Lombardo hijacked his whiskey-laden truck on its way from Canada to Cleveland. When Lou confronted him, threatening to retaliate, Lonardo threatened him with death.

Ignoring the warning, Lou and his men grabbed Lonardo's truck as it rumbled near Cleveland on its way from the complicated route from Cuba.

I have wondered why he would create his own death sentence. I know he was well aware that the Mafia did not make empty threats because he had hidden in his house for weeks after his run-in with Lombardo. Maybe he was one of those people who seek out danger, climbing mountains or jumping from airplanes or racing cars at two hundred miles per hour? Is surviving danger the only way they know they're alive? I wanted to know because I share his genes, because I'm curious about him, and because I have confusing feelings of anger for him not loving me enough to stay alive and be my father.

Meanwhile, my mother's sister, Della, and her husband, Addie—short for Adolph—came with their baby, Lucille, for a visit from their home in Philadelphia. Apparently, Lou, no doubt suffering from cabin fever, figured he'd be safe outside if he wasn't alone, and took Addie with him to the pinochle game in the back of Tabac's cigar store. As if Addie's presence could save him. As if anything could.

Lou and Addie were home in less than an hour and were ambushed in my parents' driveway. They fought heroically, desperately, wrestling the knives out of the assassins' hands, even cutting them, knocking them to the ground, until the killers had to shoot them.

Awakened by the gunshots, the two young wives ran downstairs in their nightgowns to their husbands, bleeding on the ground, their screams and wailing were so wild their next-door neighbor, George Conroy, ran in fear to check on his children.

Hearing the sound of police sirens, the neighbor ran to the window downstairs where he saw several police cars in the middle of the road, a couple of ambulances, maybe nine or ten cars parked on both sides of the street. His wife, Alicia, joined him at the window. "Say," she said, "is that a body being carried on a stretcher to the ambulance? Oh, and there's another one."

They saw their neighbors among the chaos—the Larsons, Bonds, and Hucks with coats over their night clothes against the chilly November night, and watched as the police sent them so far back from the action that they slowly returned to their homes. Now George and Alicia saw *The Cleveland Press, Plain Dealer and Cleveland News* trucks with several men emerging, the bright flash of cameras adding to the chaos. "They must be reporters," George told his wife, as more people arrived—men and women. Some seemed to be crying. A chilling light rain had started, making the street slick, adding to the misery of people and traffic on the narrow street.

George went to the phone and called Bill Larson, his next-door neighbor.

"Hey Bill—what's going on outside there?"

"Don't know. The cops made us leave."

"You didn't pick up any information?"

"No—well, the lady—the one crying—she's Rosen's sister. Never did find out about anyone else."

So the Larsons and the Conroys and Hucks and the other neighbors, and everyone else in Cleveland, had to wait for the newspapers to find out what had happened.

2

All I Know is What I Read in the Newspapers
Will Rogers

Ten years later, when I was twelve years old, I asked Kenny, my sixteen-year-old brother, why our mother would never answer questions about our father. She was at work that day and Kenny and I were home from school on spring break. Since he could drive a car and yell at our mother and have a job in a warehouse, I figured he would know. "All she ever said was that he died of pneumonia."

"Pneumonia?" He looked up at me from his breakfast of cereal and toast. "That's a good one. He died of murder—they were murdered." He said that he was six years old and remembered the night of the murders: the police and reporters and weeping relatives.

I was shocked at the information and, at the same time, I wasn't. His words felt both strange and familiar—after all, I was there, wasn't I? Upstairs in my bed? Hearing the screams and sirens?

"*They? What do you mean they?*" I asked.

"Uncle Addie was killed with him."

"Uncle Addie? Who is Uncle Addie?"

"Aunt Della's husband." He put his spoon down and looked at me. "Tell you what," he said. "Go downtown to the public library and read the newspaper's account of Uncle Addie and our father and the murders."

"Which newspaper?"

"All three."

"How do you look them up?

"By the date. They were killed on your second birthday."

I didn't know what to think about two murders on my second birthday. And who was this Uncle Addie? I had never heard of him. Why were they murdered? I looked at Kenny eating breakfast but I didn't ask him. I didn't want to know. I didn't want to go downtown and look up secrets. I left the kitchen sorry I had asked.

That day I had planned to go to the movies to see Bette Davis in *Of Human Bondage* with my friend, Helene. The idea of finding out more about my father continued to nag me, but sneaking downtown to look up my mother's secret felt like a betrayal. I must have changed my mind two or three times until I found myself on a streetcar going downtown.

The librarian told me that the newspaper archives were in the lower level of the library. I took the short elevator ride down, which stopped with a bump. The room was smaller than I had expected, with long wooden tables and chairs. The light was soft and tan like old sepia pictures. A librarian sat at a desk. Four or five people were scattered among the tables. Mostly men. No children.

I approached the librarian with a racing heart. She looked up at me, but I had lost the power of speech. Maybe because I wasn't supposed to be there. It reminded me of how I used to stutter until my mother said in a raised voice, "You don't have to say b-b-b!" And I stopped. I stopped stuttering! Forever. My mother scared me into normal speech.

Now, the librarian said an impatient "Yes?"

After a long moment, I said, "May I see The Plain Dealer, The Cleveland Press and The Cleveland News for the week of November 14th, 1922?"

She was tall, a bit overweight and as pale as if she slept down here. Without saying a word she got up and disappeared into the door behind her. I stood, waiting and waiting; she finally emerged with a pile of newspapers on long poles, then she led me to a nearby table.

The Cleveland Plain Dealer, of November 15, 1922 was on top of the pile with a front-page headline:

LOUIS ROSEN AND ADOLPH ADDELSON LAY IN ROSEN'S DRIVEWAY RIDDLED WITH KNIFE WOUNDS AND BULLETS

Their bodies were found by their wives in the driveway of Rosen's home. Although Rosen was known as a "big time" bootlegger, informants told police that the other victim, Adolph Adelson, who was married to Mrs. Rosen's sister, Della, had merely been visiting his in-laws with their baby from their home in Philadelphia and had no connection to bootlegging activities. Louis Rosen knew they were after him. Informants said for the past month he hadn't left his house.

Rosen is survived by his wife, Florence, and two children, Kenneth age seven and Babette will be two years old today. The birthday party planned by her mother and father will not be held. Adelson was an accountant in Philadelphia where he specialized in income taxes. He served in the navy during the war and was a graduate of Wharton School of finance at the University of Pennsylvania. Besides his wife he is survived by his year-old daughter, Lucille.

There it was, my family's secret, on the anonymous, bloodless, print of newspapers. And there *I* was, twelve years old and alone, the last to know about my own family.

There were sob stories on the front page, background stories of the bootlegging business. An artist's drawing of the killer's getaway car—a Peerless with the curtains closely drawn. A picture of my mother's sister, Della, and her husband, the unlucky Adolph. Another artist's drawing of my father and uncle being shot as they lay on the ground. A picture of my mother holding my two-year-old self; her face is softer, younger.

I had to reread those paragraphs again and again, trying to find a way out of my confusion. It's not that I couldn't understand the words—of course I did—but my incomprehension had the confusion and power of a dream. My father took an innocent man to his death? Destroying the man's family? How can that be? And my mother was part of the killing story, wasn't she? It was her sister who became a widow at the age of twenty-five because of my father? And how can *that* be? People in families don't go around getting each other killed. Or do they? And what about the baby of the canceled birthday party? The newspaper said it was me, but I didn't want her to be me. I wanted a father who didn't get murdered with Uncle What's-His-Name. I wanted a mother who stayed home and cooked things in the kitchen and looked like a regular mother.

What I wanted to know was: How can a family live with so much guilt?

The headline of November 18, 1922 on the front page of *The Cleveland Press* blared:

BLAME SLAYING OF TWO TO RUM WAR. HUNT RUM KING IN ROSEN MURDER. ROSEN'S PARTNER DISAPPEARS.

Halfway down the page there is a photograph of a mob milling around the funeral home with the caption:

Because of the large crowds at the funeral home, Rosen's hearse had to unload the casket from a rear entrance. In the hope of getting some clue to the killers, detectives mingled with the large crowd of mourners and curiosity-seekers who attended Rosen's funeral.

In my mind's eye I create the day of the funeral. I am put to bed for my nap by a big lady. But I can hear people in the kitchen and living room—some are weeping. I can't sleep. Something is wrong. Something big. I stand up in my crib and scream. No one comes. My baby cousin, Lucille, and six-year-old-brother, Kenny, join my cries.

Finally, I am taken downstairs. Grown-ups in dark clothes stand around whispering to each other. There is a cloying smell of sweet pastries, the clatter of dishes, ladies in aprons are busy in the kitchen. One of them gives me a cookie. She is crying. I have never seen a grown-up cry before, and I start to wail. A man picks me up. His face feels scratchy. He takes me to my mother who sits in a big chair. She is wearing a black hat with a veil that covers her face, and it scares me. I pull the hat off of her head. I can't stop crying. I feel her heart pound under her dress and hold on to her until someone takes me away to wipe my runny nose. I am two years old.

I imagine my mother sitting *Shiva* as the arriving mourners wash their hands from a pitcher on the front stoop in the ancient Jewish funeral ritual—as if this was a benign death and you could wash off the wreckage.

I wondered if my father's killer was among the mourners, imagining two or three men putting their fedoras and coats on the racks provided by the Berkowitz Funeral Home. In my mind, they approach my mother offering their clean murdering hands to her in sympathy. Feeling a merciful numbness my mother accepts their handshakes. She is not afraid. She has been a bootlegger's wife long enough to know that as long as they keep their silence, widows and children are sacrosanct. No one will harm her unless, of course, she breaks the code and reveals the killer's name, which she knows to be Joe Lonardo.

The mourners fill the large, proud living room. My mother looks around for my brother, a tow-headed blue-eyed boy, but he has already escaped into the back yard our daddy had equipped with swings, a jungle gym—even a child-sized car. Earlier, at the burial, as the male of the bereaved family, the Rabbi had him throw a child's handful of dirt into the freshly dug grave as the Rabbi muttered the *Kadesh*.

Discovering that I was born into a family of murders and secrets, I believed that my father was up in heaven watching over me with his gun, keeping me safe because he loved me. I'd wander home from the library alone in the dark night, or hang out in the drugstore, looking at magazines until the manager turned out the lights, opened the door, and told me to go home. But I liked the library the best. The books on the shelves were my friends, their stories waiting to take me out of my life. I loved the long shiny tables. I loved pulling down one of the lined-up encyclopedias and the way its weighty pages transformed my confusing, baffling world into the wonder of an orderly alphabetized universe. The walls of soft colored volumes were windows of stained glass, and the reverent hush of the people around me were worshipers in the church I never got into. I'd daydream that Miss Allen, the librarian, was my mother as she handed me a book she thought I'd like, or told me to lower my voice or that my books were overdue or to go home because the library was closing. I liked Miss Allen. I loved Miss Allen. When she put on her coat and turned out the lights I wanted to go home with her.

I remember sitting on our apartment's cold stoop at night looking at the stars and daydreaming, waiting for my mother to come home. It's hard to believe how attached I was to her during my childhood, with how desperate I was to get away from her at eighteen—desperate enough to even marry the wrong man. When she left me with relatives when I was three or four, I was afraid she wouldn't come back for me and imagined she was pushed on the subway tracks by a crazy person. Or she was mugged and shot. Her office building was on fire. She stumbled and fell down. Someone called an ambulance to take her to the hospital. But which one? Which hospital? If she had been unusually late, I sat myself cross-legged at the front door and waited in an eerie silence.

(Among other effects that I have worked through in therapy, is a lifetime of associating a person's unexpected absence with death. I know that the person is simply late, of course, I know that. But on another level I think he or she died.)

I liked the times she went out on a date, though, because I took the fifty cents she had left me to have dinner at the deli and had a banana split at Miller's Drugstore and flirted with the cute guy behind the counter instead. Once when I was nine or ten years old I drove the car the two blocks to the deli, but I didn't know how to turn it around toward home. Some man in a suit and tie opened the car door, pushed me over, got in, and turned the car around.

He looked at me. "How old are you?"

"Twelve, almost thirteen," I lied.

"The hell you are. Where do you live?"

"On Overlook."

"Okay, I know where that is, drive the two blocks slowly and carefully. Get yourself home and stay there," he said. "If you were my kid I'd give you the lickin' of your life. You could have killed somebody! Where are your parents?"

I shrugged. "Out."

"Go," he said, getting out of the car.

I put the car in gear and headed home, still warmed by the man's scolding. I liked it. I loved it. It made me feel important—like someone cared about what happened to me. My mother never scolded me—no matter what I did—not even when I skipped school. She was always at work, or on a date with Marvin, or sleeping on the couch, or reading the newspaper, or saying, "I'm exhausted. I'm exhausted."

Or we were moving again. It was as if we were running in place because each new apartment looked like the one we had just left. Years later I counted them; we moved fourteen times in nineteen years—from the time I was born until I married Nate in 1941.

My mother is as clear to me as my father is confusing. Although she was widowed in her twenties, she never remarried, as if seven years of marriage to my father was enough for a lifetime. After my father's death I remember watching her put on a short glittering dress and fancy earrings fit for a princess that I learned in later research was a flapper dress. Flappers changed their long skirts for short glamorous dresses, drank bootlegged whiskey in Speakeasys, danced the Charleston, rolled their stockings to reveal their thighs, rejected having children. She bobbed her hair and flirted provocatively—even with my high school dates when I was sixteen years old. Since she had grown up in an orphanage with bars on the windows I didn't begrudge her those years of Flapperdom, because The Great Depression was waiting in the wings. The fun and games would be over for her, and my brother and I would have our mother back.

She didn't look like anyone's mother. She was too young-looking, too chic—even then, even during The Depression. She would add a scarf or a belt or a necklace left over from her flapper heyday and look like a page in *Vogue*. Back then mothers stayed home, but she went to work in high heels and bracelets; people thought she was my sister. She fascinated my friends with how un-motherish she was, how charming, vivacious, flirtatious—how much like a girlfriend. But I wanted her to be like their apron-clad moms who didn't scare and excite and hypnotize and then slip away like ether. I longed for safer, plumper arms, the smell of dinner cooking in a warm kitchen. My mother brought home cardboard cartons of Chinese food for our dinner, smelling of her office and stale perfume.

She had been given a thorough religious and academic education in the Jewish Orphan Home. Every morning the children would be brought into the auditorium for the director, Dr. Wolfenstein's lecture. He taught The Ten Commandments, each one examining its role in life, forbidding, among other sins, stealing, false witness, adultery. (Years later, I wondered how she handled the fifth: *Honor your father and mother.* In an orphanage? Please.) Knowledge and law were examined for relevance in life, along with guidance and advice. I know all this because she lectured me as Dr. Wolfenstein had lectured her about leading the ethical life, telling me, "Don't do what I do, do what I say."

Reading everything, remembering everything she read, she would tell you more than you wanted to know about anarchy. About the League of Nations and the carnage of the First World War. John L. Lewis and Leon Trotsky. She loved getting into political arguments with people because her head was stuffed with esoteric details just waiting to spring on some poor Republican who would soon find himself hopelessly out-matched by her facts, her passion, her verbosity.

I liked listening to her—the problem was that she talked and talked about everything except what mattered. I wanted to know what it was like growing up in an orphanage. As an adult, I had read *Inside Looking Out* by Gary Polster, a professor at Ursuline college who had researched and written a book about the Jewish Orphan Home during my mother's years there, from 1900 when she was three years old to 1913 when she graduated at fifteen at the top of her class. The book described the children's constant hunger as they stole food from each other, from the orphanage's kitchen, from climbing over the fence to the neighbors' ice boxes. When caught by the Director, Dr. Wolfenstein, they were given demerits. With a certain number of demerits, they had to eat all their meals standing up for one week. Shame, humiliation, and guilt were the primary disciplinary techniques.

They slept on cots, one hundred to a dorm. I wanted to know about my mother's hunger and demerits and punishments. About her friends—were the children close with each other or too de-prived and wary? And her teachers—did any teacher take an inter-est in her? Or were they too busy, tired, and underpaid? There were five hundred boys and girls in an under-staffed under-financed or-phanage, unable to feed even basic nutrition requirements.

From *Inside Looking out* By Gary Polster:

Breakfast was a kind of gruel-like oatmeal served without milk or sugar on chipped tin plates," Coffee was a slop of stale ground beans and

hot water. Each child was given a slice or crust
of stale rye bread which was thinly swabbed
with margarine. A tin cup of milk was saved for
boys who looked tubercular. It took the orphans
about three minutes to finish their meal.

And where did she go when she boarded me to Aunt
Jane's apartment when I was fourteen? I guessed it was to be
with Jack Beatty in a hotel because she got all flirty and flushed
when he joined us for dinner at the deli. Jack Beatty worked in
my mother's office. I bet he was married. I hated Jack Beatty
because I had to take two streetcars to get to school every
day, requiring a long wait at a street-car stop in the freezing
Cleveland weather. I didn't complain to my mother, or refuse
to go there, because I believed that without Aunt Jane I would
be in the orphanage.

I wanted her to talk about my father. Did he cheat on her
as Uncle Mike had said? Was he brave or stupid in defying the
Mafia? Did she love him? Did he love her? And where did she go
when she sent Kenny and me to live with relatives? And who with?

I wondered if she knew of Lou's life of bootlegging and
gambling, but from what I understand about my mother it
wouldn't have stopped her from marrying him. When she was
a year old her father died of consumption; at the age of three
she was abandoned by her mother. Lou Rosen was considered
a catch for anyone, especially for an orphan girl, the envy of
all who knew her. Handsome as a movie star, he drove a shiny
Winton, his father owned a prosperous bakery, he had money
in his pocket.

My Uncle Sid told me that Lou was a generous friend who helped many relatives financially, a good father who was crazy about his children—especially me. Curious and still confused I wondered about his childhood, his relationship with my mother.

My aunt gave me some pictures. In one Lou is a dark-eyed child on a tricycle. Another shows a muscular youth standing with his brother Marvin in front of a horse and wagon from the family bakery. In another he stands serenely in a handsome tan suit, looking for all the world like a gentleman of banking or the law. His lips are thick and sensual, his eyes deep-set. He is a beautiful young man.

I imagine him on a date with my mother, say, in 1915 or 1916. He squeezes the horn of his Winton as five or six children gather around and touch its gleaming black surface. He is impatient and squeezes the horn again. He leans against the car, jiggling his leg. His energy crackles the air. He gives each of the children, who are now climbing all over the automobile, a nickel and shoos them away. Finally, my mother comes out. He rushes to her at the doorway, takes her arm and almost runs with her to the car. She is wearing her sister Mabel's good blue dress and her mother's feathered hat. She knows there will be hell to pay but now my mother is smiling as she proudly let's herself be handed into the splendid automobile by Mr. Lou Rosen.

I can't help wondering what my father's future would have been like if he'd lived. He was only in his twenties—couldn't he have matured and outgrown his restlessness, and stayed alive to be a father to Kenny and me? Or would he have been a leader in the Jewish Mafia? Of course I know that he might have been in jail or hiding from his enemies or the police. I know that. But

I daydreamed that he was a player in Las Vegas with equity in Bugsy Siegel's Hotel Flamingo. I would be there with my dad, in charge of booking the celebrities for the shows, a casino princess in beautiful clothes and jewels with my father, the king.

3

The Party's Over

In 1929 The Dow lost ninety percent of its value in one day, and my mother was among millions of others who lost everything. I could feel her fear—it was in the air like a presence, as if it had a weight, as if you could touch it. She worked for the City of Cleveland which was so broke it paid its employees in 'script,' which looked like Monopoly money and was just about as useless in the grocery store. So on paydays, too humiliated to try to buy groceries with play money, she put my eight-year-old self in the car and sent me into grocery stores to ask if they took script. When one of them finally said "yes" she'd go in and buy groceries. Potatoes were a penny a pound; gas was ten cents a gallon; a loaf of bread, a nickel. You could buy a new house for four-thousand-one-hundred dollars.

The suicides were legendary. Banks had only enough money to honor ten cents on the dollar because they had used their depositors' savings without their knowledge to buy stocks. There was such a run on banks that they closed their doors and you couldn't get what money you had. Men and women dug through garbage cans and stood in bread lines and soup kitchens. Families evicted from their homes ended up in the streets sleeping in parks or sewer pipes. Some families built Shantytowns made of cardboard, tar paper, glass, lumber, or anything else they could find. Called Hoovervilles, after President Herbert Hoover who was blamed for The Depression, they were scattered all over the country. Some Hoovervilles were as small as a few hundred; others in New York and Washington D.C. held thousands.

Unable to pay the rent in our apartment in Cleveland Heights, my mother moved us to East Cleveland into a building her boyfriend, Marvin, owned and provided with free rent. Marvin Stone was a former municipal judge who was called "Judge" Stone for the rest of his life. I liked Marvin—he was nice to Kenny and me and in our life for years until he suddenly, out of the blue, married someone else. True to my mother's secrets I never knew who dumped whom, ending their long relationship. Years later when I was married to Nate, I saw him and his wife in the country club dining room, but he pretended he didn't see me. I got a good look at his wife. My mother was better looking.

Since we were unable to continue paying my grandmother's rent and expenses, my mother reluctantly moved her in with us, saying she hated her. Which made me nervous—you aren't supposed to hate your own mother, no matter what.

But her presence made us all worse. A policeman brought Kenny home after catching him driving our mother's car. He was fourteen. My mother had more of her temper fits. I rarely showed up in class and came home later than ever. Kenny began tormenting me, chasing me with the bugs I hated, making a monster face at night in my room with a flashlight under his chin, doing anything he could think of to torture me. He hit me. I didn't tattle on him when my mother came home from work because she said "don't aggravate me" so often it was ingrained in my head with the not so subtle threat of being sent to an orphanage as she had been. Also, if I told, Kenny would hit me all the harder when we were alone. Still, we each had our roles in this new constellation: mine was to keep the peace and not aggravate my mother; hers was to go to work, get paid, come home, and not kill herself. Kenny at fourteen had the unfortunate role of surrogate adult male. Tall for his age, and worried looking, he was sometimes taken for our young-looking mother's husband. Which he hated. Grandma was utterly silent and disconnected, unless she was swearing in Yiddish. She was supposed to do the cooking for us, which she did, but her food gave me a stomach ache.

Years later, researching for this book, I understood my mother's anger at Grandma.

During the years she was in the orphanage her mother never visited her or her sisters. Not once. Not in twelve years. On the day my mother graduated Dr. Wolfenstein pointed to a stranger in a brown coat and feathered hat and said, "She's your mother."

She and her sisters—Mable at seven years old, Lilly at four, and my mother at three had been running wild, dirty and hungry in the streets. Some good neighbor reported my grandmother's neglect, bringing a Mr. Morrison from the Jewish Orphan Home who collected them in the horse and wagon and took them to the home. I imagined my grandmother running after the wagon crying, "My Babies! My Babies!" like in the movie *The Kid*. But what I know of my grandmother, she simply watched them leave from her grocery store window.

❊ ❊ ❊

Franklin Roosevelt was elected in a landslide in 1933, in the depth of The Depression. I was eleven years old and, amazingly, he was still in office when I was old enough to vote for him. I remember my mother sitting bent to the radio, scarcely breathing, hanging on to every word of what the President called his 'fireside chat.' His melodious voice was intimate, as if he was speaking only to you, as if you and the world were safe as long as he was there, talking to you on the radio. The expression on my mother's face was transformed, softer, almost adoring, as if listening to a lover, or maybe to the father she never had. I liked the fireside chats, too, because she was always in a good mood, smiling and chatting, waiting for the broadcast and finally turning on the radio in anticipation. I liked her good moods and tried to create them by not aggravating her or complaining about the walk to her office on sixth street and almost being knocked over by the force of the icy wind blowing off Lake Erie. The problem was that her office was in City Hall, which was on the lake. Then we would have dinner in a cafeteria, which I also hated, filling my tray only with desserts, hoping my mother would make me take back. But she never did—she just wrapped them up to take home, and I'd have a dinner of chocolate cake and oatmeal cookies.

She wasn't alone in her worship. Roosevelt was elected four times, and it would have been five if he hadn't died first. Like a shot in the arm of the sick economy, he created Social Security and founded thirty-two new government agencies, among them: the Public Works Administration (PWA), The Emergency Banking Relief (EBRA), and The Works Progress Administration

(WPA). As much as he was loved, there were those elites who hated him, and called him, "A traitor to his class."

Still, in some unexpected way, it was a better America. There wasn't the polarizing of Washington or the abyss between the rich and middle class and poor. We were all in the same boat; looking out for each other like family; united in mutual struggles, losses, and misery. Even Al Capone opened a soup kitchen.

The contrast between that time and this is obvious, disheartening, and baffling. The elegant experiment of democracy's success, that is America's unique story, and the envy of the world is being dismantled by unprecedented dishonesty and incompetence.

Surely, we do not need the disaster of economic failure like The Great Depression to find America's soul.

4

War!

When the Japanese attacked Pearl Harbor on December 7, 1941, Nate and I were celebrating our upcoming wedding. Hosted by my Aunt Gertrude for friends and family, there was a buffet of delicious food, beer and whiskey, flowers from my future in-laws, toasts and animated talk—a party!

Suddenly, there was a loud knocking on the door—we thought someone in the apartment building was complaining about the noise. Nate opened the door to the next-door neighbor who had had his radio on.

The room went silent. Nate and I looked at each other in confusion, bewilderment. "War!" someone yelled. People who had been drinking sobered up; some began gathering coats, others sat down, stunned. Nate and I thanked Aunt Gertrude for the party and left; we had some decisions to make. Absurdly, ashamed, all I could think of was that the war broke up my engagement party.

We sat in the car. "We should cancel the wedding," I said. "People will understand."

"Yes," Nate said, "but I could be drafted any day, which would mean it could be years before we could marry."

Thinking of living with my mother for years changed my mind instantly. "Let's go ahead with the wedding," I said. "I changed my mind," I said.

So, right or wrong, that's what we did. We got married. I had just turned nineteen—what did I know? Only that marriage to Nate provided an escape from my mother. I was still upset about the night before when, not to be outdone by her sister Gertrude's engagement party, she had invited Nate and me to Gruber's for dinner, one of the most expensive restaurants in Cleveland.

"Mom, Gruber's is too expensive. Let's go to Aurora's for spaghetti."

"No way. What am I? A poor relation or something? We're going to Gruber's. Make a reservation for Saturday at seven o'clock."

Later, I blamed myself as much as my mother for what happened, because I knew better. But her invitation—as if she was a normal mother—was irresistible, and I made the reservation.

Gruber's was *the* place to be for dinner on Saturday night. My mother in her element swept into the restaurant in her good beige silk and high heels and her hair upswept like Betty Grable's, looking for all the world like the sister of the bride. We were led to a table and given menus. My mother studied the menu and recommended the vichyssoise or shrimp cocktail and the beef tenderloin as if she dined at Gruber's every night. She selected a good Bordeaux from the wine list, offered cocktails. She was animated, gracious, charming. I watched her proudly, but warily. I didn't know how long this new mom would last. We had Manhattans. We had shrimp cocktails. Fillets with a mushroom sauce, wild rice, and baby carrots. We had salads. A waiter passed warm rolls. My mother toasted our happiness with her fine Bordeaux. For dessert she swept away my protests and ordered a Baked Alaska. By now my pride had changed to panic—she had easily spent over two months' salary. When a waiter brought the bill I could hardly breathe.

But I had underestimated her. My dressed-up mom sat on her hands and looked around. She took her lipstick and compact from her handbag and carefully touched up her lips. She put a cigarette in her mouth and leaned forward to Nate's match. The leather folder with the bill discretely tucked inside lay there and I saw what was coming. My fiancé was getting stiffed. And with no money of my own—I turned my paychecks over to my mother—I sat red-faced and helplessly mortified as Nate finally opened the folder and paid.

"How could you!" I screamed when we got home. "How could you do that to Nate!"

"He can afford it," she said, pulling off her dress.

I took a deep breath. Calm down, I told myself. Nineteen days! In nineteen days I'll be married and away from her forever. Or so I thought.

"Babbie!" my mother said when I came home from work. "We're having a wedding dinner for forty in a private room at the Alcazar Hotel! Aunt Sophie is taking you shopping for your wedding dress tomorrow!"

I sat down in my coat. "You didn't."

She opened her eyes wide. "Didn't what?"

"How could you!"

She looked innocently around the room.

"You went to them. You begged."

"The hell I did," she snapped. "I don't beg."

"What would you call it?" I said, bitterly.

"They owe you. I merely reminded they owe you."

"That must have gone over big."

"Listen, isn't your Uncle Marvin a rich big-shot? Doesn't he have a chain of bakeries? Your CPA Uncle Sid got started in business with our money. All those years of The Depression I'm alone raising two kids. Not a helping hand from them. Not a penny or a telephone call or a dinner invitation. He can pay for a lousy wedding dinner and some flowers. Big deal. They owe you. It's high-time they gave you some help.

I have to admit the wedding was lovely—my gown and veil beautiful, that my mother made Aunt Sophie buy. The ceremony was held in the Euclid Avenue Temple, Rabbi Brickner officiated. I floated down the aisle, a virgin bride, on Uncle Sid's arm. He handed me over to Nate and sat down.

Elegant in his trousers and cutaway, Nate gripped my arm. His face was red and he was swaying slightly. I smelled whiskey on his breath. He smiled at me, but it was the grin of a husband who turns into a hideous stranger in a bad dream. Although the Rabbi began praying in Hebrew all I heard was the sound of my mother weeping in her seat in the front row. These were not a parent's sentimental sniffles; they were loud wrenching sobs as if I were about to be executed. I was unnerved, embarrassed, scared. Why is she crying like that? Did she know something I didn't?

Afterward, we went to the Hotel Alcazar for the wedding dinner. The table, fragrant with flowers and scented candles was lovely. There were gold-edged place cards and a tall wedding cake with a bride and groom on the top. Dinner was roast beef with wild rice and asparagus—dessert, slices of the spectacular wedding cake, it's magnificence worthy of the daughter of her family's bakery. My mother was a radiant hostess in a short beaded and fringed dress from her flapper days. Nate's mother was dressed in a bright blue silk that was a size too small for her ample curves. She was short and good looking, with pretty blue eyes. Nate and I sat at the head table with my mother and Nate's parents. His mother called him "Sonny Boy" adoringly, and kept trying to engage him in conversation which he ignored. There were toasts to the bride and groom and sentimental speeches from my uncles—my father's siblings—as if they hadn't ignored me my whole life, as if we weren't strangers to each other.

Later, during my psychoanalysis I had the insight that my existence reminded them of the guilt, shame, and loss they felt at Lou's life and murder, taking his innocent brother-in law with him.

Expecting Nate to be drafted at any time, we rented a furnished apartment in the Commodore Hotel near the Case Western University campus. It had a bedroom, living room, and tiny kitchen. We were the first of our friends to get married, so our apartment became a gathering place for those who, like Nate, were waiting to be drafted.

At first, there were at least eight or nine young men and

their girlfriends—sometimes more—coming and going at all hours of the afternoons and evenings. They were all young enough to like hanging out in our apartment away from parents. They brought beer—we supplied the pretzels and chips. No one got drunk; it was as if fighting in a war required sobriety, their past carefree drinking an innocence lost.

In time, many in our group were drafted, including Nate, whose departure surprised me with feelings of relief. Barely past our honeymoon he had already exhibited a trigger temper. After Nate left, our group was reduced to five: Frank, Phillip, Billy, Benjamin, and Jacob. Each time one of them left for war I felt an unfamiliar stab of sadness and foreboding.

Frank was deferred because of low vision, which was ironic because he was the most macho, the most eager to get in the fight. He was short—maybe five feet nine—but his muscular swagger was what you noticed. Training like a prize-fight-contender he lifted weights, ran five miles a day, did push-ups and used every machine in the gym. He was one of the regulars, arriving daily to the apartment around four o'clock, so when he didn't show up for two or three days his absence was felt keenly. Over the next weeks we learned that he was driving an ambulance in Europe for the Red Cross.

Philip was fiercely opinionated about the evil of violence, even during wartime we got tired of his rantings and ravings. He was so smart and articulate that no one wanted to argue with him, and he just went on and on. Even I could see that he would be a total misfit in the army. Julie, his girlfriend, a rather plain young woman, was always with him. A few years older than Philip, she was as quiet as he was talkative—you could barely get a word out of her. We did learn later from one of his buddies that he'd had a nervous breakdown and was given a Section Eight (Discharged from the military due to mental problems). To our surprise—no—astonishment—Julie left him; she just didn't seem to be the type of woman who would do that. Reminding me that you can never *really* know a person.

Billy was so good looking, and charming you couldn't help forgiving him for his flagrant womanizing, bringing a different girlfriend with each visit. One evening, when Judith asked him to take her home, he told her to take a cab without looking up from his conversation with Philip's date. Which I thought was beyond rude, bordering on cruel. The youngest in our group, at twenty, he was a serious pianist of classical music, could beat everyone except occasionally Philip at chess, and was given a full scholarship to Case Western University. But Billy was spoiled— first by his parents and then by girls. And by his movie-star looks—blonde and blue eyed, six-foot-two, slender and fit. But although the group's heaviest drinker, he never brought any beer, never offered to help clean up. He was captured by the enemy during the Battle of the Bulge in January, 1945 and spent the war under harsh conditions at a prisoner of war camp. To no one's surprise who knew him, the Germans did what his parents and friends didn't or couldn't, and he came home after the war a different man. He still played the piano, he still beat most every-one at chess, but he had changed. He was unsmiling, solemn, and although he had lost twenty pounds, there was a kind of heaviness to him. Even the charm was gone, as if it belonged to another time and place. As if he had no interest in charming anyone.

I tried to get in touch with Billy after the war, but the few leads I had led to a dead end.

The first thing I noticed about Benjamin were his eyes; they seemed too hard in one so young. But when I learned more about him I understood. His father was in jail—convicted of a white-collar crime that was a sort of pyramid scheme that lost millions of his clients' money. His father had accumulated huge debts from his sentencing and his mother's lavish spending. Eager to get away from his parents Benjamin enlisted in the army as soon as war was declared. His father sent us a brief letter notifying us that he was killed on D-Day, June 5, 1944 on Omaha Beach. We published his death in a *Hello Again* column of increasing casualties. We were heartbroken.

I liked Jacob the best. He was a jock, working out with weights every day and running five miles. With black eyes and black hair and a swarthy complexion, he looked like the bad guy in one of those cowboy movies set in Texas or Mexico. After Nate was drafted, the two of us would sit on the couch and talk. He was a good listener—attentive and understanding. He told me about his plans for college after the war, about his parents, and his sister who was brain damaged from a car accident in which she was driving after drinking. A passenger died—a six-teen-year-old girl. His family, he said, never recovered from the guilt and shame. Not to mention the lawsuit.

"I'm just glad she's unable to comprehend the tragedy she caused. From what I know about her she wouldn't be able to handle it. It just about ruined my mother, and my dad sort of disappeared, staying away from the house more and more." He leaned back and closed his eyes. When he opened them they were wet. "You're the only person outside of the family I've even mentioned her name." He looked at me. "You're so young I don't know why I trust you. it's even hard to believe you're married."

"I'm nineteen."

"Exactly."

Every time I was reminded of my marriage I felt a stab of surprise. Being married surprised me. It had been only a few months since the wedding and during much of the time Nate was away in basic training and then overseas.

I fantasized about an affair with Jacob. Candlelit dinners. Summers at the beach. Dancing at the Pavilion at Mentor. Weekends at Cedar Point. Sleeping together. Introduced to sex on my wedding night, I now understood its preoccupation and power—even its obsession. But this was 1942, when there was a cultural denial of sexuality that was part England's Victorianism and part America's Puritanism. The sexual revolution of later decades was impossible to predict and astonishing to those like myself who lived through the transformation.

Benjamin and Philip were playing chess Sunday night as Frank left. Anna, Jacob's girlfriend, had gone home. The room was quiet.

"I can't concentrate," Phillip said, pushing his chair back. "I feel so damn useless."

"Maybe we should send each guy a box of delicacies and cookies." Jacob said.

"The war would be over by the time we could make enough boxes for everyone," Billy said.

"Let's write to them," Philip said.

"Same problem. Too many of them and not enough of us," Billy said.

"Not if we write the same letter," Jacob countered.

"Yeah, like a newsletter," Philip said. "Or a bulletin."

"Let's make a list of the names and addresses of guys we know," Philip said. "Army, Navy and Marines."

"Use my mother's address for their reply," I said. "She's the only one we know where she'll be."

We had thirty-two names and addresses of servicemen for our first mailings, titled *Hello,* receiving about ten or fifteen replies an issue. By the end of the war our mailing list titled *Hello Again* reached five hundred men in the armed forces.

HELLO AGAIN

SWAP SHOP FOR NEWS

YOU TELL US.

WE TELL YOUSE

We copied cartoons from *Esquire Magazine*; we had a column called *Cleveland is Talking About* with local news and sightings of mutual friends in favorite bars and restaurants. We reported on babies and promotions and furloughs. We wrote articles about life on the home front like rationing, and stories about their sisters, wives, and mothers at work in factories. The letters we received from the servicemen were sad and funny, boring and fascinating; there were homesick letters and censored letters with blacked out paragraphs; letters about how much receiving *Hello Again* meant to them; letters about finding brothers and cousins and friends because we printed their addresses.

Nate was the first to be drafted; Philip and Billy about
the same time; Benjamin followed two weeks later and Jacob a
week after that.

Now alone, I gave up the Commodore apartment and reluctantly moved the *Hello Again* headquarters to my mother's
apartment. Where else could I go? And there I was, living with
her again, as if she pulled me back by the sheer force of her will.

Now, with the founding men—Billy, Benjamin, Jacob
and Philip drafted, we recruited army wives Angela Grower and
Elaine Marcus; Fred Colander, a retired sixty-year-old *Cleveland
News* reporter; we even had a fund raiser, Dick Monroe, who got
us the money for color, professional design, and postage. The
staff changed every few months; the army wives would leave to
join their husbands on furlough, or to get a needed paying job.
Surprisingly the changes in personnel didn't seem to matter to
Hello Again—new people simply picked up where the others left
off. The one constant presence was my mother; she was like a
rock around which people came and went month after month,
directing newcomers and once or twice single handedly doing
what had to get done to meet deadlines—managing to mimeo-
graph the *Hello Again* pages in her office, stuffing, stamping, and
addressing envelopes, and lugging them to the post office. She
deserved all the praise she got, including mine with a surprised
appreciation of a side of her I had never seen.

When our mailing list reached more than five hundred
servicemen we were stopped by the War Department from
publishing their addresses and names. We were told that the
list could provide valuable information to the enemy. We did
continue to publish without the addresses.

Over the years copies slowly disappeared and we lost a uniquely personal history of the war straight from the service men's intimate expressions of endurance, comradery, fear, homesickness, excitement, danger, and dread. And always, always, the enemy. Reading between the lines of the letters I could see their pride and their anxiety. I could see the war's demands that they grow up overnight.

From the time I was born until I got married my mother moved us from one apartment to another fourteen times in eighteen years. So it was no surprise when, in July of 1944, she decided to move to New York and had located a job as secretary in a New York import-export company. She insisted that I go with her, and in those days I was no match for her will. She rented an apartment on East 72nd Street—a sublet.

After the Japanese attacked Pearl Harbor and Roosevelt declared war on Germany and Japan, life as we knew it was transformed. Men under fifty were rarely seen, gas and most necessities were rationed. The changes seemed so swift it was as if aliens had captured all of our young men while we slept. If you saw a man say, in the post office queue or cooking hamburgers in a diner under 50 years old he was looked at with suspicions, the way Japanese American families were suspected of sabotage and put into camps for the duration of the war.

New York in wartime was like a village. There were only a few cars on the road; the manufacture of automobiles had been replaced with the building of airplanes and tanks and munitions.

We got around on buses and the subway and our own two feet.

Most foods and fuels were rationed. We were issued ration stamps for meat, sugar, fat, butter, vegetables, fruit, tires, and clothing. Thousands of women went to work as electricians, welders, and riveters in defense plants. The once crowded bars were virtually empty—joining the bartender and his few customers was like joining family. Everyone had a loved one in harm's way overseas, connecting us in a frightening, exhilarating way. We talked like old friends about the latest war news, about the bravery of our ally, England, being bombed night after night. Although it took the raid on Pearl Harbor to get the U.S. in the war, Churchill's speech to end America's isolation remains famously inspiring to the U.S. and allies. One night, a regular in the bar, a man of sixty or so, had memorized Churchill's New World speech and recited it:

> "*We shall go on to the end, we shall fight in France, we shall fight on the seas and oceans, we shall fight with growing confidence and growing strength in the air, we shall defend our island, whatever the cost may be, we shall fight on the beaches, we shall fight on the landing grounds, we shall fight in the fields and in the streets, we shall fight in the hills, we shall never surrender…until in God's good time, the new world with all its power and might, steps forth to the rescue and the liberation of the old.*"

We told our stories to each other, skipping our fears. My new friends did the same as if, like rationing, being positive was a patriotic duty.

The mantra "The war effort" was spoken everywhere—from the impatient line at the grocery store to the frustration of rationed gas to losing places to servicemen on trains, buses, restaurants and hotels.

We wore hats in those days—you weren't dressed fashionably without one, and I got a job modeling hats on the fifth floor of 711 Fifth Avenue. Changing hats in a black dress and heels on Fifth Avenue was an improvement over my first job in the Seventh Avenue garment district modeling dresses and suits. My boss, Sam Feldman, was a short, Type-A personality, who was the mild Dr. Jekyll in the showroom with buyers and the crazy Mr. Hyde yelling in the stock room with me. At first his yelling upset me but soon I saw his yelling at me was simply the way he communicated to everyone—the receptionist, whoever was on the telephone, his wife who worked part-time, the deli delivery kid with lunch. Everyone, that is, except the buyers, to whom he said the same pitches and jokes that the rest of us heard so often we knew them by heart.

When the war was over and Nate came home, I told my boss that I was going back to Cleveland with my husband.

"You're WHAT!" he yelled. *"Cleveland?"* As if it were Siberia.

I had worked for Sam long enough to understand that to him, every place that wasn't New York was Fargo, North Dakota.

"Yes," I said. "Cleveland."

"My God, you're going to be a provincial housewife in *Cleveland!* he yelled. "You'll never last!"

It took twenty-five years, but he turned out to be right. But it wasn't Cleveland, it was the husband.

5

Discovered by Freud

Riddle There is a woman with three beautiful children, a twelve-room home, a fifty-five-foot yacht named after her, a country club membership, designer clothes, live-in help, and four-star travel who is desperately unhappy. How can she be unhappy? What is wrong with her? Is she spoiled? Crazy? What?

I know the answer to the riddle because that woman was me. I didn't realize it then, but my unhappiness was caused by being emotionally abused by my husband. Like most abused people I thought his abuse was my fault; I was a bad wife, mother, friend, person. And to make matters worse, I felt guilty—how could I be so lucky and so miserable? What was wrong with me? Maybe I really was crazy as my husband frequently reminded me.

❋ ❋ ❋

"I'm not tall enough for you," Ralph said on the phone, "but would you go out with my friend Nate Silverman?"

I had met Ralph at a party the night before. He had a wide mouth, light-colored eyes and a head full of thick black hair.

"Why doesn't he call me?" I asked.

"Dunno—maybe he's bashful."

"Call me back tomorrow. I'll tell you tomorrow," I said.

I hung up and called my friend, Lydia, who knew everyone.

"Lydie, should I go on a blind date with Nate Silverman?"

"Yes!" she said. "He has a red convertible!"

And from such trivia my life was changed forever.

Nate definitely was not bashful. He pursued me with the arrogance of the spoiled rich-man's son that he was. Nate was drafted into the army a few months after we married, so that we barely knew each other when he left for basic training at Fort Benning in Columbus, Georgia, and then overseas to Fogio, Italy. I lived the drama and romance of war like a teenager, which, after all, was what I was. Playing myself in a forties war movie, my husband was at war saving us from our enemies while I bravely kept the home fires burning.

I was shocked into reality when President Truman ordered the atom bomb dropped on Hiroshima and Nagasaki, and the drama and romance of the war changed to horror in a matter of hours. It was as if I had grown up overnight.

The bomb ended the war, Nate came home, and I had another shock when he loudly called me irresponsible and greedy for using some of the War Bonds he had sent home. We were on a train going to Cleveland from New York, where he had disembarked from a troop ship. If I could have stopped the train at that moment, I would have left him then and there. But the train kept rattling along on the tracks, and I began to rationalize his furious outburst; he was fatigued from the long voyage home on a troop ship crowded with thousands of soldiers; coming home after two years at war is a difficult adjustment. Surely, he didn't mean what he said; surely, he'll apologize.

As it turned out, his outburst was only the beginning of twenty-five years of the same. My determination on the train to leave him never returned, which made me see that marriage to Nate had been another one of my fantasies. Divorce never occurred to me because I began to believe that I deserved his abuse, and moreover, would be no match if he contested a divorce. Besides, we had three children: Eric, Steve, and Lisa.

After Nate's father turned over his lucrative furnace and air conditioning company to Nate, we bought a house…that Nate picked out, and a dog, a Schnauzer…that Nate picked out…

While doing research for this book, I discovered my 1956 journal. Here is the entry from January 21 that sums up my marriage to Nate.

My New Years' Resolutions for 1956

1) Please my husband
2) Learn how to play golf
3) Don't be so unhappy
4) Learn how to drink at country club parties without throwing up: More than three I've wound up on the bathroom floor.
5) Don't be so unhappy
6) Don't throw up on the yacht "Babette" during rough waters
7) Learn how to flirt.
8) Don't be so unhappy

Without money of my own, or family, divorce was unthinkable in my world. Helpless and hopeless, I allowed myself a delicious little fantasy, but only when I was in the bathtub with the door locked. *Nate has a girlfriend and wants a divorce, which means that I get enough money for allowing it.* And this one: *Nate dies and I'm a rich, beautiful widow and FREE!!* I like that fantasy the best because I don't have to kill him.

One morning, after my children were in school, my friend, Elizabeth, came over, pounding on my kitchen door.

She often dropped in but this time she was very agitated—something about finding out that her husband was seeing another woman. Elizabeth and I often commiserated with each other about our unhappy marriages but this seemed worse. After listening to her story I got an idea.

"Elizabeth," I said. "You don't have to be unhappy! You can go to a psychoanalyst for help." And then a revelation. A revelation! *I* could go to a psychiatrist.

Believe it or not, I got Dr. Herman's name from the Yellow Pages under the heading "Psychiatrists." His was the first name so I called him. I had to wait almost two months for an appointment, and by the time he greeted me in his waiting room I had changed my mind several times. But there he was, standing there in a good suit, looking for all the world like your best friend's dad or maybe an accountant. He was slender, not tall, in his fifties, which I thought of as old (I was thirty-three).

He asked some questions; Can I commit to fifty minutes every day? (Yes) The fee is $25 a session. How did I feel about that? (Okay) What did I expect from therapy? (That it could change me into a better person so my husband would not have such disdain) What did I know about the process of psychoanalysis? (Very little)

Every day at two o'clock I would lie down on the couch in Dr. Herman's office, pull my skirt down over my knees and ramble on for fifty minutes. Sometimes I sobbed repressed tears into the silence. Once I fell asleep. Although I found Dr. Herman's determined silence frustrating—at times infuriating—I came to understand that he kept himself a blank screen on which I could project my fantasies and transferences for his interpretation.

In 1955 going to a psychiatrist meant that you were crazy. After all, Freud had only been dead for sixteen years, which made me a pioneer. So, in secret shame, I never told a single soul, which at times was awkward given my daily appointments with Dr. Herman. I'd say I had a dentist appointment; if anyone became suspicious of my pitiful lie they didn't say. But years later, my friend, Elise Carter told me she thought I was meeting a lover.

After five years of therapy, including repairing the damage inflicted by my mother and husband, Dr. Herman was moving to Atlanta. We shook hands and said goodbye. He told me to call him at any time, but I doubted that I would—for the simple and complicated reason that I wasn't the same woman who began psychoanalysis five years ago. And if five years of daily fifty-minute sessions seem excessive, in the concept of their life-changing achievements, it is a moment. In addition, what is not generally known is that when you work through the transferences, dreams, the conscious, and unconscious mind successfully, the psyche continues emotional, intellectual and spiritual growth.

❊ ❊ ❊

"Why not take a college course or two?" Dr. Herman had said. "Get your feet wet?"

"I'm not smart enough for college," I told him.

"What makes you think so?"

"My mother."

"She told you that you weren't smart?"

"Not exactly. She said that she was smart and it was better to be like me—good looking."

"How old were you?"

"Fourteen or fifteen."

"Your mother was wrong," he said.

"She pulled me out of eleventh grade for a modeling job."

"That was wrong, too."

I sat up and looked at him. He was serious. He said my mother was wrong. He said I could go to college. After a year of psychoanalysis he knew me better than my mother ever knew me my entire life. His belief gave me the courage to take a GED Test to determine the ability to handle college-level work. To my surprise I passed.

My first course in college was Western Civilization, a terrible choice. My eighteen-year-old fellow students had just come from high school classes; at the age of thirty-three, I had arrived from my kitchen and motherhood and wifehood. As I tried to follow the professor's lecture I was seriously afraid I was going to faint or throw up; he could have been speaking in Russian for all I was able to understand. My first grade was a D; after studying like a medical student I brought it up to a B by the end of the semester.

And, behold, for my second semester I took fifteen hours and got all A's. Feeling liberated from my former self, I liked the new me, which was really the old real me rediscovered. It was like seeing color after black and white, hearing live music after recorded, eating fresh vegetables after canned, reading literature after pulp. I was beginning to experience the deep pleasure of being authentic.

An essay I wrote in my Creative Writing class, "Confessions of an Unpublished Writer," was accepted by *The Saturday Review* in 1961. I didn't know it then, but it was the beginning of my life as an author, publishing seven books of fiction and non-fiction, many in my 80's and 90's. And this book at the age of 97.

6

The Times They are A-Changin'
Bob Dylan

We landed a man on the moon. Protestors of the Viet Nam war drove President Lyndon Johnson from office. A moral awakening of Civil Rights sent James Meredith to become the first African American to enroll in the University of Mississippi. Sex was hidden in the fifties and celebrated in the sixties, helped by the game-change of the birth control pill. Searching for American communists McCarthy was ruining American lives with his demands for the names of Communists in government and Hollywood.

The sixties turmoil was in part a reaction to the dutiful, rigidly conforming fifties.

Housekeeping Monthly
May 13, 1955
"The Good Wife's Guide"

1. Have a delicious meal on time for your husband's return. This shows him you are concerned about his needs.

2. Rest so you'll be refreshed when he arrives. Touch up your makeup and put a ribbon in your hair.

3. One of your duties is to be a little gay and a little more interesting for him.

4. Clear away the clutter. Dust the tables just before your husband arrives.

5. Catering to his comfort will provide you with immense personal satisfaction.

6. At the time of his arrival eliminate all noise of the washer, dryer or vacuum. Encourage the children to be quiet.

7. Be happy to see him.

8. Greet him with a warm smile. Let him talk first. Remember his topics of conversation are more important than yours.

9. Don't greet him with complaints and problems.

10. Don't complain if he's late for dinner or even if he stays out all night.

11. Make him comfortable. Have him lean back in a comfortable chair or lie down in the bedroom. Have a cool or warm drink ready for him.

12. Offer to take off his shoes. Speak in a low soothing and pleasant voice.

13. Don't ask him questions about his actions or question his judgment or integrity. He is the master of the house. You have no right to question him.

14. A good wife always knows her place.

The guide is a laughable relic, as outdated as a dinosaur. But at the time it was a powerful force in women's lives. I should know because I was there, and it was no laughing matter.

Having grown up with an independent, single mother I was able to somewhat resist "The Good Wife Guide." I didn't take Nate's shoes off or put a ribbon in my hair, but as a wife in the 1950's I didn't escape the cultural pressure and did try to please him. But Nate's expectations of my being "a good wife" in addition to his verbal abuse was, for me, a lethal combination.

Seven years later, in 1962, a free-lance writer no one had ever heard of by the name of Betty Friedan published a book called *The Feminine Mystique.* Wondering if other women felt as unhappy in their lives as she did, she interviewed her former classmates at a Smith College reunion. Discovering that many women were also discontented in their limited, unequal roles as wives and mothers, she went on to conduct countless interviews with housewives, psychologists, editors, and professors. She found that countless American women were suffering in silence from a mysterious sense of discontent that Friedan called, *The Problem That Has No Name.*

I read the book into the night. I read it again with a profound feeling of relief. I was being heard! I wasn't alone! There were a great many of us! Betty Friedan *got* it!

I had no idea that this book would start the second wave of feminism, or change the lives of women and men forever. I only knew that the book revealed that I wasn't crazy or alone in my discontent and confusion.

At the beginning of my analysis, divorcing Nate was unthinkable. At its conclusion, being married to him was equally unthinkable. Therapy had changed the balance of blaming myself for Nate's abuse. Revealing that I wasn't stupid after all repaired my damaged self-image and lifted the burden of guilt I carried for twenty-five years for being a bad wife and mother and terrible person. It became inevitable that I could no longer be married to Nate and with Dr. Herman's support I found the courage to proceed with a divorce.

When it became known to our friends that we were getting a divorce, a woman who I'll call Barbara came over late one evening. Nate had moved out; the children were asleep. It was one of those miserable cold and windy nights with intermittent rain that Cleveland was known for, and I couldn't imagine what would bring Barbara out on such a night.

"I want to talk to you," she said as I opened the door to her.

I led her into the den, a small room, and sat down on the love seat. She sat next to me without taking off her coat and took my hand.

"Please don't take what I'm going to say the wrong way," she said.

I waited.

"It's because I love you," she said.

I braced myself, wishing to high heaven I'd not let her in the house. It was ten thirty at night for God's sake.

"Our friends at the club are upset over your divorce," she said, "but I'm the only one who will tell you the truth."

"Oh?" I said. "And what would that be?"

"Honey, I understand that you're unhappy so I'm going to tell you a little story. Remember when Ed and I went to counseling?"

I didn't but said I did.

"Well, the counseling didn't work and we were on the edge of divorce." She let go of my hand and sat back with a small smile." But we're still married and our children's home and family didn't get destroyed. And you know why?"

I shook my head.

"I took a lover," she whispered. "And that's what I want for you."

I stared at her, not sure of what I just heard.

"And if you're judging me," she went on, "just keep in mind that when there are children divorce is immoral. We know that. You know that. Everyone knows that."

I didn't know whether to laugh or cry over such pitiful values.

But eager to just get rid of her, I thanked her nicely for her—ahem—advice while counting the days until I was divorced from her and her friends' mistaken lives.

The divorce turned out to be merely a matter of appearing before the judge with my attorney and my friend, Anita, who had accompanied me. I was asked a few questions: *Is this divorce uncontested? Yes, Your Honor. Are children being contested by you or their father for custody? No, Your Honor. Is this divorce what you want? Yes, Your Honor.*

"Divorce granted," the judge said.

And twenty-five years of marriage were ended.

My lawyer and I shook hands—Anita gave me a hug, and we left the courtroom.

"Let's go for coffee," she said. "There's a place down the street."

The lawyer had declined to join us.

Sitting down at a table in the coffee shop, I felt tears fill my eyes and run down my face.

"I know how sad you must be," Anita said.

"Sad?" I said, wiping my eyes. "Anita, these are tears of relief."

So I was surprised—no—*astonished* by strange, new feelings of joy, bliss, and happiness. It was like I was dreaming; it was like I was drunk; it was like I was awakened from a nightmare to a kind, benign world. (Everyone is so *nice!*). I not only got my own bed—I got my own *life*.

I discovered dating. It was interesting to have men in my life for the first time. Looking back now, I see those first years after my divorce as the adolescence I never had. There was the testing of myself against this amazing new world and a new way to live, learning the pleasures and problems of the dating world, learning from my mistakes, learning how to be alone, learning about myself. I raced around from job interview to job interview in a burst of creativity energy and was hired as a columnist for *The Cleveland Press*, and as host for a Sunday morning television interview-show

In 1968, reading *The New Yorker* a small advertisement caught my eye:

> The Educational Development Center (EDC) is an academic rehabilitation program for under-achieving students who have failed to remain in college because of poor grades. Created by Robert Pitcher, Dean of Students at Baldwin Wallace College, it is located on the campus of the college in Barea, Ohio.

Intrigued, I wondered if a program like that would help my son, Eric. I let myself feel hopeful for the first time in months—ever since he flunked out of college nothing I did—or didn't do—helped.

He had a love-hate relationship with his father since eighth grade. Granted, that his father was very difficult, Eric had a way of making him even worse.

They were at a standoff: his father punishing him (you can't use the car until you bring your grades up) scolding him (you have a high IQ, why the hell don't you use it?) bribes ($10.00 for every A). The more his father punished, threatened and bribed, the more Eric defied him by simply going AWOL, physically and mentally, in his classes.

Meanwhile, I had called the Academic Rehabilitation Center in Berea, Ohio, and made an appointment for Eric's interview and potential enrollment. Now all I had to do was sell it to Eric and his father. Which I dreaded because they were both mules.

Nate was usually in a better mood after playing golf so I called him after his golf game on Sunday to tell him about the Educational Development Center.

"It's designed for students like Eric," I said.

"What do you mean like Eric?"

"Kids who flunk out of college like Eric."

"So he'll be with a bunch of losers."

"It has nothing to do with winners and losers. It's an academic rehabilitation program."

"He has a genius IQ for God's sake. 160! And you want to send him to kindergarten. Anyway, he'll never agree to go to that place."

"So, if he agrees to go you'll agree?"

"Okay, but he'll probably flunk out of that place, too."

I planned on taking Eric to his favorite pizza place, just the two of us. I planned what I would say about the virtues of the Educational Development Center. About his dismal future without college. He had heard it all before, of course, but this time there was help.

"Did you tell Dad?" he asked.

"Yes," I said.

"What did he say?"

I had a sudden inspiration." He doesn't want you to go there." *Okay, I lied.*

"Sign me up."

I had to laugh. After all my worry and preparation all I had to do was tell him his father was against his going. I could have done it on the telephone.

At the time Eric entered EDC over six hundred failed college students from two-hundred-fifty colleges had gone through the ten-week program after undergoing comprehensive diagnostic tests. Studying in a calm academic atmosphere, away from his father, Eric was able to access his fine mind and he thrived. Berea is near Cleveland, where we lived, and I drove there a few times to have lunch or dinner with him. I hadn't seen him as relaxed and happy since he and his father declared war on each other.

Eric completed the ten-week course on August 1st and returned to college on September 15th. Soon after he left, I got a call from Dr. Pitcher asking when I'd be available for a meeting.

"Is it a problem with Eric?" I asked, worried.

"No, no, Eric was one of our best students. I saw on his EDC application that you're a writer, and I have a project to discuss."

Intrigued, I agreed to meet with him in Berea the following Tuesday.

It turned out that Dr. Pitcher wanted to collaborate on a book about the EDC. I would do all the writing, he said, and as co-author have the option of either sharing 50% of the royalties with him or be paid weekly as we worked. I chose the salary, he produced agreement documents, which we signed and were witnessed. We started work a week later.

Co-authorship can be tricky, but Dr. Pitcher and I worked well together. We met every two weeks and he would teach me about the program—its structure, techniques, and philosophy—as I took notes. At the next meeting we'd go over what I had written for corrections and clarity. Meanwhile, I sat in on classes observing the program come to life, inspiring my work. My mission was to write the students' case histories that illustrated specific problems such as low self-esteem, confusion, lack of support, guilt, anger.

Why College Students Fail was published by Funk & Wagnalls to good reviews in 1970. There was a book party attended by former and present students of EDC, Bob's and my family and friends, and Bob's academic colleagues.

Looking through my notes to prepare for a radio interview, I reread the profiles I had written about underachieving students. I read them again. And again, something was bothering me about them—an idea that kept nagging at me and slipping away. Finally, I gave up and filed the notes away under Educational Develop Center and put whatever it was out of my mind. That night, sound asleep, something woke me so suddenly I sat up in bed, wide awake. *I got it!* I got what's been bothering me! The profile of underachieving students was similar to the profiles of underachieving women! There was the same lack of self-esteem; the same confusion about who they are and what they want and similar resentments of authority. And if Dr. Pitcher could design a program that helped students, he could design one for women, too, couldn't he? I couldn't wait to talk to Bob; it took all my willpower not to call him at three o'clock in the morning. The next day, Sunday, I called him at home for an appointment in his college office. He was curious—I rarely if ever called him at home—but all I would say was that I had an idea to discuss.

The following Monday he listened to my proposition and liked the idea as I had hoped. But as in the past, every time I'd get carried away by an idea he would drag me back to reality. Which is what he did that day.

"What about location?" he asked. "The college can't host it. And there is the matter of start-up money. Are you willing to work without compensation? Am I? Time is a consideration because of my classes three days a week. Oh, and do you have an advertising plan?"

His questions were mere details to me, doing nothing to stop my adrenaline rush. With a new clarity I knew that the key was Bob Pitcher's impeccable credentials that would give the idea authenticity and gravitas.

"If I come up with answers to your questions would you sign on?" I asked him.

He gazed at me. He took off his glasses and polished them with a tissue from the box on his desk. "How will you go about getting answers?"

"With your qualifications I'll have no problem," I said, trying a little flattery. "I just have to drop your name."

He put his glasses on. "I haven't said I'd do it."

"But will you?"

"Let me think about it—talk to my lawyer. If I design the program I'll need some kind of agreement."

"Please get back to me soon?" I asked, impatiently from my adrenaline high.

I expected to find a location relatively easy. *Ha.* The spokesperson in each of the places I called—churches, libraries, schools—reacted more or less the same. *Women? With all the problems in the world? Tell your professor to get real and focus on some real issues, not some crazy bra burners!*

My explanation and defense of *Discover Yourself* (its name evolved from my own 'self-discovery') was ignored—sometimes politely, sometimes not—but in any case, I shouldn't have been surprised. In those days women were expected to live exclusively as wives and mothers. The fact that I was ahead of my time with *Discover Yourself* was little comfort.

Reading the *Sunday Plain Dealer* I noticed a column of special events that were being held in the May Company department store in Cleveland Heights.

There was a course on flower arranging, a field day for children to visit a chocolate chip factory, a series of fashion shows, a course on how to read poetry, make-up lessons and more. It requested that for more information you contact the office of Eugene Waters, Vice President of Special Events.

It turned out that Eugene Waters of the May Company's Special Events and *Discover Yourself* were made for each other. He *got* it. Maybe because he had three daughters, or that he was raised by a single mother, he was one of those rare male feminists. Meanwhile, Eugene Waters, Bob Pitcher, the attorney, and myself worked out an agreement.

The May Company would supply *Discover Yourself* with a suite of three furnished rooms in the department store in Cleveland Heights. *DY* would pay The May Company twenty-five percent of its gross profit. Bob and I would work initially without compensation, with the hope and expectation that *Discover Yourself* would become a franchise with its financial value to be split evenly between Dr. Pitcher and myself. We signed the agreement; it was witnessed by two of Bob's students.

We had open houses weekly at which time I described *Discover Yourself* to the audience in detail, taking questions and signing up those women who wished to enroll. The open houses were usually well attended, but I found that many women came more out of curiosity than self-discovery. We usually signed up seven to eight women for a program, but after three or four months, the number dropped and I saw that the program's demise was built into its success. Like many small under-financed small businesses, I counted on word-of-mouth to recruit women. I knew the program was successful but what I didn't know and should have, was that women came to class secretly and told no one because the conventional wisdom was that she had failed as a wife and mother if she needed our courses. All of which was illustrated by the phone calls I received from a couple of husbands, each demanding that I do not accept his wife into the program. My reply was that his request would have to come from his wife.

At the end of the ten-week program, we asked each graduate to describe their experience and opinion of *Discover Yourself,* with our assurance that we would protect her identity.

From Betsy B:

I almost didn't sign up for Discover Yourself because I knew my husband wouldn't like it and I don't like to lie to him. But I did lie and I'm so glad I did because I am a different person on my way to a different life. I found all the exercises helpful, but the part wherein we discover what our values really are is what hit home for me. It showed my discipline in day to day life as a wife and mother but that I could live with joy and passion if I went back to finish my law degree. I had already completed two years in law school when I quit to get married and had children. Now, thanks to Discover Yourself I intend to go on to a law degree. I am aware that my husband will forbid it, but the Assertive Training sessions of DY have given me the tools, encouragement, support and mind set I need to make it happen. I will not let him stop me.

Thank you thank you.

From Elizabeth R.

I really liked the women in my program. It just felt good to be in an environment of strong supportive women who understand each other's desire for a different life. About Discover Yourself, I found all the exercises' interesting and certainly helpful. But when we were in the Relationship section it was as if I had been unknown to myself but in a strange way also known—the "known" part nicely buried and out of the way to accommodate, please, and satisfy my husband. I saw that pleasing him was based on fear, not love. I saw that I am no longer a frightened child, but a grown woman with a life that belongs to me and not to my husband. Since I feel the beginning of an independence that will change my relationship with my husband that I never thought possible, my future looks different. Exciting and sort of scary.

From Susanna K.

I'm not sure I like what I discovered about myself—the resentment, *and jealously especially. It's true I'm jealous of anyone with a slimmer figure, and my cousin's Jaguar. I'm even jealous of my best and oldest friend from college, because she is now in her third year of med school. In the anger section of Discover Yourself I saw that the jealousy was from my unhappy life of difficult children, a dominating husband, parents who have this great forty-year love affair, neither of whom has ever been there for me. I feel that Discover Yourself started something important and it's up to me to continue the work. I mean psychotherapy. As I write this I have no idea how I'll manage the time and money, but after a vision in Discover Yourself of what my life can be I'm determined to get the professional help I want and need. I'm thinking of asking my parents—they can easily afford it and maybe it's about time for them to finally be there for me. (This insight came from the program's training on identifying Your Goals. So thank you.)*

Well, as they say, the operation was a success, but the patient died. Although we had to terminate *Discover Yourself* after only eight months, it was not a failure because it changed the lives of most of the women who signed up for the ten-week program.

No one knew that in the future women would achieve freedom as a birthright with unimaginable choices in relationships, careers, sex, motherhood, and marriage. Even abortion became the law of the land.

Although *Discover Yourself* is gone, everything I learned of possibilities, tenacity, and hard work is still guiding me.

7

If You Want a Friend in Washington Get a Dog

"*W*hat do women want?" One of Hubert Humphrey's assistants asked me, echoing Freud's famous question, which turned out to be rhetorical because he kept on talking. I was being interviewed for a staff position as liaison to the fledgling women's movement for the 1972 presidential campaign. In 1968 Humphrey had lost his presidential run to Richard Nixon; now, four years later, he was in a race with George McGovern for the Democratic nomination for president. The campaign had flown me to Washington D.C. from Cleveland for the interview because I was from the politically essential state of Ohio, was a columnist for *The Cleveland Press,* and because Humphrey's deputy chief of staff was a friend who recommended me.

The Humphrey headquarters didn't look as I had expected. There were no pictures of Humphrey on the walls, or map of the U.S. with projected red and blue states, or phone banks, or busy important people coming and going. Besides the chief of staff's large glass-walled office and a big board room, there were six or seven men and women in their offices talking on phones and typing. (Computers had not yet revolutionized life.) I never saw Humphrey's office or Humphrey, for that matter. Later I learned that there were volunteers working phone banks and advance-people and staffers stationed in storefronts all around the country.

The assistant held out his hand when I arrived and mumbled his name, which sounded like Harry or Jerry something. He had sandy-colored hair, longish in the style of the day, brown eyes, shaggy brows and a killer handshake. He seemed distracted and young—maybe too young, I thought, for such a position. I didn't know then about the small army of political junkies in their twenties who go from political campaign to campaign year after year trying to land on a winner for a ride to the White House or a Senator's staff. They thrive on the polls, the competition, the strategies. Paid little, they sleep on friends' and political supporters' couches and feed on the chase.

Harry or Jerry sat down at his desk as I stood awkwardly, wondering if I should go ahead and sit in the other chair in the room.

"Sit, sit," he finally said. He looked at his watch, he looked at me, he leaned back in his chair. "See," he said, "I'm not sure I'm the right person for this. But I have to say that even though I'm a mere male, I do understand that the days of ladies' political teas are a thing of the past. I know that. But beyond equal pay for equal work, what do women want?" he asked again.

I had prepared for the question. "Well, for starters," I said, "we need subsidized day care and regulated workers—many children spend their first five years of life in day care. Also, paid leave for childbirth and the first months of the newborn's life. We want representation on corporate boards, women acting CEOs and in Congress, and don't get me started on equal pay. American women earn only fifty-eight percent on the dollar, compared their male counterparts." I stopped. Harry or Jerry was making a phone call. I think it was about a lunch date with someone—a woman by the way his voice dropped to a kind of purr. I longed to tell him he was rude and that he could shove his job—I longed to walk. But I didn't. I wanted this job. Badly. I wanted access to the power of the president to actually help the lives of women. I didn't know then that what they hired me to do they would not allow.

"Sorry," he said, hanging up the phone. He leaned back in his chair again and gazed at me. Then he said, "Tell you what. Go back home, go back to Cleveland, put your ideas and what you just told me in a report with statistics and methods to implement. Make your case. Have it in Artie Page's hands by the 22nd," he said, getting up. He escorted me to the door as if he couldn't wait to get rid of me.

Back in Cleveland I wrote a thirty-page report with enough statistics, numbers, and titles to make your eyes glaze over. It included a Paid Domestic Violence Leave Bill, which would give victims of violence funds to escape with their children. Also, the Violence Against Woman Act needed renewal. In addition, I proposed that the Hyde Amendment be removed from the Health and Human Services Bill because it prohibited federal funds from being used for abortions.

Reader, I got the job. Smallish salary, expenses, lodging in

The Georgetown Inn.

Harry or Jerry assigned a windowless office to me about the size of a large broom closet. Then, still distracted, still mumbling, he introduced me to the other staffers and to the deputy chief of staff by the name of Artie Page, a disheveled-looking man around fifty who needed a haircut and barely looked up at the introduction.

I went to work on a list of women's issues, researched demographics from previous campaigns—suburban, college educated, married with children, seniors, Black and Hispanic minorities, both working and stay-at-home moms. I worked on it for the better part of two weeks and then, trying not to show my pride in the thing, I handed it to Artie Page who tossed it into his in-basket like yesterday's newspaper without looking at it or me. For the second time I felt like walking out of the campaign but knew I wouldn't.

My battered pride took another hit when Betty Friedan returned my call in which I had proudly introduced myself as Humphrey's liaison to the women's movement.

"You're not going to get much help from a politician," she said.

"But Humphrey hired me," I said.

"Humphrey's a politician," she said. "Lower your expectations or all you'll get is frustrated."

Gloria Steinem was even briefer. She said she felt sorry for me. *Ouch.*

I watched as Artie Page's in-basket emptied and filled again and again, leaving my memo as undisturbed as if it had grown there.

So I called one of Humphrey's speech writers, a man named Kevin, and introduced myself and asked if I could write a few pages about women's issues and goals for a speech. He said that he'll get back to me, so vaguely I knew he wouldn't. And when I saw my fellow staffers go into Artie Page's office for a meeting without including me, I figured it was time for me to give up, back off, and go back to Cleveland, no hard feelings.

I was writing a resignation letter to Harry or Jerry explaining my departure, effective immediately—I hadn't been employed long enough, I figured, to give the customary two weeks' notice. And just then, just like in the movies, I got the phone call that changed everything.

It was Janet Coles, a freelance reporter who wanted to interview me. One of the campaign's public relations people had sent press releases to the D.C. media about my being recruited as liaison to the women's movement. The reporter didn't know how hollow that impressive title was, and I sure wasn't going to tell her. (Although the real story is probably more interesting than the one I was about to make up—namely how disinterested white male power is in improving the lives of women.) She invited me to lunch that very day, giving me the name and address of the restaurant.

"Welcome," the restaurant hostess said, smiling, as if she wasn't standing there on roller skates. A mere week ago that would have astonished me. Now, I simply gave her my name and followed her to a table as I made my way around the skating waiters amid the din of voices, the clatter of skates, smelling delicious wafts of barbecue.

The first thing I noticed about the reporter, Janet Coles, were her green, long-lashed eyes. As if in compensation, everything else about her seemed ordinary—sensible shoes, printed blouse, navy blue skirt, no jewelry. (Pants for women were forbidden in most offices in those days.) I felt almost overdressed in heels and a pin-striped suit that I had thought rather plain until I observed first-hand the reason for Washington women's reputation for being dowdy. She looked about forty or so with even features and hair a color that seemed to have given up trying to be blonde.

A photographer was at the table. He introduced himself and took a picture of me standing up and another seated at the table. He said thank you to me and see you later to Janet, and was gone.

"Isn't this a fun place?" Janet said. "I love coming here."

After ordering lunch (Janet, a cobb salad; me, a cheeseburger) and some small talk (the weather, home towns, families, restaurants), Janet Coles took a tape recorder out of her briefcase and put it on the table. "You can tell me to turn this off and go on background at any time."

She asked interesting questions and good follow-ups, she listened and took notes. After being stonewalled by Artie Page and Harry or Jerry, her interest and attention was irresistible, and after answering the first few questions, I talked and talked nonstop, unleashing streams of words on the poor woman. I talked about choice; the psychological aspects of feminism on society; the role of the family, the effect on children, the resistance of many men, and even some women; I talked about the polls showing McGovern ahead of Humphrey on women. In the process of sharing so much, I talked myself into staying on the job.

The restaurant had emptied. Janet Coles turned off the recorder. A dog was barking somewhere in the sudden quiet.

"When and where will it appear?" I asked.

"Don't know. I'm freelance, remember?"

"You mean you did this on spec?"

"Yes, but I expect it to sell to the *Post.*"

"The *Washington Post?*"

"I have two good contacts there," she said.

"Well, good luck with it," I said, thinking, it will never see the light of day because I've yet to find anyone in power interested in improving women's lives.

Janet Coles had invited me to meet her divorced brother, Paul, and he called a few days after the interview. We met at the Mayflower Hotel's Edgar Bar and Kitchen. The restaurant was crowded with the men and women of power politics—you could tell by their confidence and animation—even by their clothes: the men in well-tailored suits and silk ties, the women wearing dress and jacket outfits and suits just this side of dowdy. In Washington if you're not a lobbyist or on a campaign for an important candidate or on certain congressional committees, you barely exist. I felt like an imposter, as if I didn't belong, as if Cleveland was written all over me. Paul was a lawyer, about fifty or so, I guessed, balding with a nice smile and dimples. It turned out that we did date a few times—that is until I tired of hearing him talk about his ex-wife.

"I found her in bed with my best friend," he said. "How about that for a cliché?"

"That must have really upset you," I said.

"No," he said, "not at all," he said, as he sprinkled salt into his coffee.

My brief adventure in politics came to a stop when Humphrey lost the primary to George McGovern in the

Democratic Convention in Miami. And I—like the other Humphrey staffers—was out of a job overnight.

It's known that in job hunting it isn't *what* you know—it's *who* you know, and it was through my position on Humphrey's campaign staff and my lofty, meaningless title, that I felt optimistic about finding another job. After all, I had made friends in DC; besides, just dropping Humphrey's name would open doors. Or so I thought. *Ha.*

As it turned out, all that my so-called friends gave me were the many ways there were to say 'No.' *My son/daughter/husband/ wife/has the flu. I have the flu. I'm moving. I'm moving my mother into assisted living. I'll get back to you after my grandmother's funeral,* and so on and so forth. And that doesn't count the people who didn't return my calls. It is, after all, a simple Washington equation. You either have a prestigious job in DC or you're chopped liver.

I subconsciously postponed my call to my closest friend in DC after Humphrey lost to McGovern. Helene had been a good friend—inviting me not only to her dinner party but also to dine just with her and her husband, Larry. We shopped and lunched and attended movies together, visited regularly on the phone. I didn't think she would reject me as the others had, but I kept putting off making the call until I ran out of excuses.

Her answering machine picked up.

I left a message on Tuesday. By Saturday when she still hadn't returned my call, I called again. Don't ask me why—even as I dialed her number I knew it was stupid. When I never heard back from her it became painfully clear that there were only two kinds of people in Washington—winners and losers—and I had been both. Winners have friends and contacts whose calls are returned—losers are ignored.

I spent the next few weeks chasing job interviews, getting lost in Washington's diabolically circular streets due to my bad sense of direction, and wound up in tears and in dangerous neighborhoods. I knew that by law government agencies must advertise available positions. The truth, I discovered too late, was that such jobs are actually almost always already committed to a chosen applicant while naïve people like me run around like dummies on wild goose chases for jobs that don't exist.

I did finally get a job, but not through anyone in D.C. My friend, David visiting from Germany, called me from the airport on his way home. He had run into a friend, he said, who had just left the Beatrice Brooks Public Relations Agency in D.C. and there was possibly an opening there.

I thanked David for the lead, looked up the Brooks Agency address and hurried to its office.

As it turned out, Oscar, a tall skinny man in his forties with a head full of premature white hair, hired me after a five or ten-minute perfunctory interview. It should have made me suspicious, but I was too happy to be relieved of the job search and to have settled somewhere.

The place occupied offices, a reception area, and a large conference room. There were pictures on the walls of political celebrities scripted affectionately to Beatrice Brooks. Oscar led me to a desk in a room with three or four other desks, all unoccupied. He nodded briefly, mumbling what sounded like, "Welcome to the glue factory." Or, "Welcome to the new trajectory." Wildly different, I know.

I sat down at the desk in the empty room. The place was eerily quiet, there were no footsteps or voices or even the clatter of typewriters, as if fear or stress or dirty secrets had soaked up all the oxygen. Oscar had said the firm was understaffed but it felt more like vacated. Then I heard the staccato *click click* of three-inch heels and the appearance of a small blonde woman with the stretched youthful face of a surgeon's knife, who could be any age between fifty and seventy. She wore a tight beige dress, gold bracelets, rings, earrings, and the aforementioned stilettos. The overall effect was more Vegas than D.C.

"Welcome," she announced, holding out her hand. "I'm Beatrice Brooks but you can call me Beatrice—everyone does." Her voice was nasal, a little shrill. "Our workday starts promptly at nine with a staff meeting in the conference room at which time you will meet the staff and receive your assignments. And she was gone.

The next morning, I came to the office early, thinking vaguely that I'd figure out whatever it was that made me uneasy about the place. It was just past eight-thirty and a man, apparently the building superintendent, was unlocking the office door.

"Another new one," he said, when I approached, shaking his head.

"Another new one?" I repeated stupidly.

"Man, this one needs a revolving door."

I stared at him. Of course, that was it.

"Good luck," he said. "I think you're gonna need it." And he went down the hall to the next office, his keys rattling in his hand.

I wanted to go down the hall to the elevator. But out of curiosity, I went into the conference room and sat down. Two men and a woman came in at the stroke of nine, as if they had been watching the clock outside in the hall. The woman, pale, gray-haired, in rimless glasses looked to be somehow misplaced, looking more like a teacher rather than a P.R. agent. The two men could have been father and son, although I learned later that they weren't related. The older one was actually better looking than the younger one—tall and slender, graying nicely at the temples, deep-set blue eyes. The young one looked like a scholar or researcher, pasty-faced, as if hours were spent indoors bent over work. I was about to introduce myself and get their names when Beatrice and Oscar came in and the older man looked at me and put his finger to his lips. That eerie silence again.

Beatrice sat down at the head of the large table carrying a file folder and yellow legal pad. "Good morning," she said, looking around the table as if there were people sitting in the empty chairs.

"Margaret, your report, please."

The pale woman said, "I have a press conference scheduled for—"

"Margaret, when you make a report, you must first state the name of the client. I told you that last Tuesday. Remember?"

"Yes, okay," she said. "The client—"

"Margaret, I asked you a question. Do you remember?"

The pale woman looked confused for a moment. Then she said, "Yes, I remember."

"So if you remember, why didn't you name the client?"

Margaret, no longer pale had turned a rosy pink. "So, I guess I forgot."

"You guess you forgot. Not very professional, are you?"

I squirmed in my chair. The man sitting across from me lowered his eyes.

"I'll just have to take over," she said sighing deeply. "The client is The Residential Equipment Company. Your mission was to save the reputation of the CEO, Michael Williams after he got caught in an affair with his secretary."

"Beatrice," Margaret broke in.

"Margaret, I'm talking. Do not interrupt me when I'm talking. Please." She began writing on the yellow legal pad as the room fell into that eerie silence. "His company just went public," she went on, "and the stockholders are up in arms trying to get rid of him. Williams has his supporters but the tabloids are writing about the boy genius and his girlfriend secretary."

She sat back in her chair and twirled the pencil in her hand. "What, Margaret, is your plan for my client?"

Margaret now looked close to tears. "My plan is to set up a press conference at the Washington Press Club where Williams, with his wife at his side, will apologize not for the affair, which he will deny, but for the appearance of an affair in his and his secretary's travel to professional meetings and so forth and so on."

"What else?"

"I'm working on pictures in the print media of Williams, his wife, Carol, and two children." She sat back and looked expectantly at Beatrice.

But all Beatrice said was, "Today is Friday. Have pictures placed by next Tuesday." She looked at her watch. "We'll break for twenty minutes."

But I had had enough—not for twenty minutes—but for the rest of my life. I grabbed my handbag and left in flight, passing the elevator, running down five floors as if I were being chased, guilty of something, feeling daring and powerful and free.

Which lasted about forty-eight hours, until, there I was, confronted with my joblessness again, feeling like a misfit in Washington and in my home town of Cleveland, which is why I left in the first place. I was right back where I started, in full circle.

So what's-his-name whose marriage proposal I had declined a year ago began to look pretty good when he called me. We began to see each other again, one thing led to another and another and we got married and it was a mistake and we got divorced.

It wasn't Jim's fault—he was a decent man. But I married him for the wrong reasons, which is why I feel guilty for the break-up. I had hoped I could figure out how to make the marriage work, but it was like trying to define the undefinable, like love.

8

There are Five Rules for a Happy Marriage but No One Knows What They Are

*I*f this was a fairy tale, Prince Charming would now appear on his white horse to rescue me. After all, I was without a job or friends with my only option a return to Cleveland that would give satisfaction to those who said I would fall on my face in Washington.

I knew my life was making me a little crazy, because there he was, Prince Charming, smiling at me, six-feet-two, blue-eyed and handsome. We happened to be on the same embassy tour and when he asked if he could take me home, still in fantasy land I was saved, chosen by Prince Charming as his bride to live with him in the castle.

He did take me home that evening, and he did ask me out for the following Saturday night as I hoped he would. We dated often after that, dining in restaurants in Georgetown and Bethesda; going to favorite bars, the movies, and to meet each other's families. It was all so wondrous I didn't know if I was falling in love with a fantasy or a man. That is, until alone in bed, or in the shower, or driving to a job interview, words of cold enlightenment began whispering in my ear: "Be careful what you wish for," it said. "He has seven children," it said. "Do you really want seven stepchildren?" it said. And what about religion? He is a devout Catholic and I'm secular and Jewish. Besides, after two divorces, another failed marriage is absolutely totally out of the question for me. I do not want to be a woman who failed at marriage three times. And if those differences aren't enough what about our backgrounds? James grew up in a normal family as a church-going, straight arrow—Navy pilot, corporate executive, eagle scout. My background was filled with murders and secrets. He was a widower with a long marriage that lasted until his wife's death; I had been married and divorced twice.

James had obliquely talked of marriage lately and I had a hunch his proposal was coming that night at dinner. I felt wretched to have to decline. As I made the sauce for the salmon I went over and over what to say, but nothing seemed right. Setting the table there were delicious aromas wafting from the kitchen, from the roses on the table, and the scented candles, as if a setting for talk of marriage, not the end of a relationship.

He appeared on my doorstep—half an hour early—with a big grin and an armful of flowers. Pulling me over to the couch he got down on one knee and exclaimed, "Marry me, marry me, I love you!"

All I could manage was a small, "I'm sorry..."

"What? What did you say?"

I shook my head. "I'm so sorry," I said again.

He got up. "But I thought—you said—I thought you loved me."

"Oh, but I do. I love you."

"Do you have a husband somewhere?"

I had to smile. "No."

"Then why?"

"We're too—too–different."

"Different?" he said, looking puzzled.

"We come from totally different worlds."

"Okay, so what's the problem?"

I was out of rebuttals. Besides, I was crying.

"I don't understand you," he said; there was an edge of anger in his voice I'd never heard before.

All I could do was cry.

He handed over his handkerchief. "Look," he said, "differences in a marriage can be a good thing—can't it? I mean we can learn from each other."

"It's not just the differences," I said, wiping my eyes. "It's that you don't know enough about me and when you do, you'll regret marrying me."

"I know enough that I'd never regret marrying you."

"My father and uncle were murdered," I blurted out, watching his face.

"Go on", he said calmly.

"Don't you want to know why"? I demanded. Why was I angry?

"You'll tell me why when you're ready," he said.

I didn't know whether to hit him or throw my arms around him.

"I've known you for a year," he said, "and I thought I understood you. I was wrong."

"You weren't wrong. You just don't know the story."

"I love stories," he said. "Tell me a story."

"My father was a bootlegger," I said. "He ran whiskey down from Canada in a truck and sold it to speakeasies."

"Prohibition was a mistake. Practically the whole country broke the law," he said.

"Yeah, but the whole country was smart enough not to get in a fight with the Mafia," I said.

That got his attention. "The Mafia?"

"The Cleveland Mafia boss—his name was Lonardo—hijacked my father's—Lou's—truck. And warned him that if he retaliated, he'd be wacked."

"Wacked? What is wacked?"

"Mafia-speak for killed."

"Okay, you told me the story. Let's get married."

"Let's have dinner," I said with a smile. I understood in that moment that part of me wanted to marry him—the part that was my heart.

We ate in silence. Or rather I ate in silence. James kept up a running commentary—the salmon was delicious—the wine a perfect match—you're looking especially lovely tonight—I've got a business trip coming up to Switzerland, maybe you'd like to come with me? And on and on he talked, filling the silence with observations, a couple of jokes, descriptions of colleagues he had traveled to China with. I pushed the food around on my plate, unable to eat because of the lump in my throat. There was no mention of marriage in his monologue, as if I hadn't just been crying on his shoulder. I liked listening to him. I liked that he didn't pressure me or sulk; it was as if he knew me. He spoke without judgment, as if taking me from my secrets and lies and shame to a different history. I didn't know how it happened the way it did, but looking at him across the table I felt a rush of love so swift and hot it reached my bones, my heart. Our differences were still there but seemed to melt by the heat, or were unable to hold up under the onslaught of the love I was feeling; or it was simply that I could not—would not—lose him. As it happened, the power of love continued to overcome our differences for thirty-six years.

James wanted to be married in the Church; being secular I had no problem with it but we worried about the church's position regarding my two previous marriages to Nate and to Jim. After going to a nearby bar for toasts and finger crossings and courage we met with the priest in the Georgetown University Chapel. Questioning each of us separately about our ages, children, backgrounds, religion, and previous marriages, he said that since my second marriage was made while my first husband was alive it was not recognized by the Church. And since my first husband had since died, I was now a widow and free to marry in the Church.

We were married by Father Gavagan, the ceremony attended by our families, after which we had a beautiful dinner in a private room at the Mayflower Hotel.

The excitement and romance of our wedding and honeymoon made it easy for me to distance myself from my worries. I moved into James' house. Tommy, the youngest of the seven, was still home; the others were scattered around the country on their own. Cooking for the three of us while trying to find my way around the kitchen, feeling an urgency to leave this house for my own home, calling real estate agencies, finding my way inside the super market. Could this be a key to a successful marriage I wondered—to be consumed with the ordinary; the everyday-ness of being alive?

It took us a long time to find a house we both liked. When I liked a house, James didn't, and vice versa. Our real estate agent showed me four or five houses until I liked one enough to show James. It had a great location near the Washington Cathedral, three bedrooms and baths, a den, two fireplaces, and lots of character.

"What do you think?" I asked James in the car after the agent took us through the house. I couldn't tell if he liked it or hated it. If he played cards—which he didn't—he would make a great poker player. You never knew what he was thinking.

"I like it," he said. "Let's make an offer."

I nodded.

"What's wrong?" he said, looking at me. "I thought you'd be happy we finally found a house."

"It's not that," I said wiping my eyes. "Just an upsetting memory."

He pulled the car over, turned off the engine and took my hand. "Talk," he said.

"Well," I said, blowing my nose, "I was reminded of looking for a house with Nate after the war. Available houses were rare in those days, and I had heard of a house coming on the market in Shaker Heights that we both knew and loved from being guests there many times. But every time we asked the real estate agent to show it to us, she changed the subject. Finally, I got an idea, and did a bit of research. And there the house was, among the *Cleveland Plain Dealer's classified* section's listing of homes were the words, *available to churches;* code for *not available for Jews.*"

"I had no idea," James said, shaking his head.

"Anti-Semitism is two-thousand-years-old and thriving," I said. "I saw the newsreels about the concentrations camps and Germany's systematic murder of six million Jews. And I'm still in total shock."

"But this is America, not Germany." James said.

"Yeah, that's what the Germans said in 1938."

"I still believe in America," he said.

Before I was married to James I thought I knew about love—you know—desire and excitement. Flowers. Gifts. Romantic dinners, jealousies. But what did I know? Books and movies were the only places I had found love—certainly not from my mother and Nate.

James' love was a revelation, changing my world from orphanhood to a worthy participant in the human family. With him I felt a previously unknown level of trust, of safety, of rooted contentment. Away from him, I felt pain from somewhere in my body I didn't know existed.

I understood what sustained him. I understood the importance of religion in his life; he understood my secularism. And although he would have liked to share his religious life with me he never asked me to convert to Catholicism—not once, not in thirty-six years.

He was agreeable about everything; in fact, we never fought with ugly words to each other. I learned in my marriage to Nate that hurtful words are as damaging and lasting as physical blows. Maybe more so, because they leave no physical evidence for support and proof to family, police, the courts, or doctors. James' method was smarter and more effective. He would listen quietly to my complaint without arguing, and then do exactly as he had pleased in the first place. He knew the most important thing was to listen.

We had been married for months when I realized that I had stopped worrying about our differences. Not that we didn't have any. James asked me not to read the newspaper at the breakfast table or in bed when he wanted the light off so he could sleep. I asked him to organize the stuff in his messy home office and car. Over time I came to see these differences as just the normal adjustments of married life. There were also similarities on a deeper level of our emotional histories. We were both raised by difficult, possessive mothers, and we both left home the first chance we had: James with his bride immediately after college, and me a month after I turned nineteen. We also shared the same values of kindness, compassion, independence, and an ethical life: James' from his church teachings, and me second-hand from my mother's religious training in the Jewish Orphan Home.

On a daily basis, I saw how James' religion went beyond attending Mass to a way of life. He read the Bible every morning. At a party or reception if he noticed someone standing alone—maybe a person of color or someone older or someone younger or "different" in any way—he would introduce himself and then stay with him or her, starting an authentic and lovely conversation.

He taught me that the greatest gift you can give to anyone is to fully accept who he or she is.

As the Vice President of an oil company James traveled the globe. Beginning with our trip around the world on our honeymoon, he introduced me to people and countries I could have only dreamed of. Once on a trip to Madrid, Spain, a lawyer James knew, who was on the staff of a Sheik, invited us on the Sheik's yacht.

After being helped aboard we were greeted by the Sheik, a bearded, dark-eyed man of medium height who could have been any age between forty-five and sixty. Wearing slacks, a navy-style jacket with a silk scarf folded at the throat, and a sea-captain's hat, it was as if he was trying for Western elegance, making me think, absurdly, that he was playing dress-up. He led us to one of the dining rooms, which turned out to be far away. I don't know how big the yacht measured, but according to the distance to the dining room it was quite a measurable size.

The dining room was large, too, but its size was softened by the mauve-colored sofas in the room. The windows looking out to the sea were draped and swagged in a sheer purple fabric, trimmed with fringe; the floor was covered with a beautiful Oriental rug in reds and purples. There were fifteen or twenty other guests—Saudis and Americans. We introduced ourselves to each other, standing around a long table laden with delicacies. A waiter offered drinks and I had the best wine I ever tasted. Some of the men were Saudi princes who were also in Western garb. The Saudi women were dressed from diamonds at the throat to sandals at their feet in the latest Italian and Parisian fashions. When I complemented one of the ladies on her dress—a green silk with a pleated skirt that moved nicely when she walked, she told me that coming home on their private jet from a shopping trip in Paris, she always changed in the bathroom into a Berka, transforming herself into an obedient Muslim woman.

❋ ❋ ❋

"I'll have a glass of Chardonnay," I said the following night to
the waiter, thinking of the great wine I had had the night before
on the yacht. The Sheik had invited us for dinner in his mansion
and we were sitting in the living room with the other guests.

"No, you won't," the lady sitting next to me said in her
French accent. I knew her from the night before on the yacht
because she was so arrogant when I spoke to her in my pitiful
French. I didn't want to sit next to her at the dinner but there
she was, next to me, showing me my ignorance that the Saudis
forbid the use of alcohol. That is, unless they were on the yacht.
Or maybe it was my dress that made her dislike me, which, in all
false modesty, I admit was better-looking than hers.

Dinner was announced and we were led outside to a large,
beautifully landscaped patio where the women and men were
taken to separate tables. After a dinner served course after course
of delicious Middle Eastern food there were grand fireworks of
exploding colors in the black sky. And then we were taken on a
tour—a Saudi teenager had been assigned to James and me as
a guide around the mansion. She led us to the ping pong and
billiards room, an elaborate gym, and a bowling alley! There was
a theater with its rows of comfortable chairs that could easily
seat fifty.

Offered soft drinks and a chair, I was happy to accept— my
shoes were killing me. I discovered that high heels were not meant
for tours of mansions with bowling alleys. We were joined by the
guests we had met on the yacht. As soon as we sat down someone
started the jukebox, playing middle eastern music and a beautiful
belly dancer appeared from somewhere and danced for us. More

food and drink were produced, which I had to decline because my clothes were shrinking just hanging in the closet.

The next morning, the Sheik called us at our hotel offering his jet to fly us to the Seville airport at eleven o'clock for our flight home. It was now nine-thirty, so we raced to pack, check out of the hotel, and get a taxi to the Madrid airport. We followed the Sheik's directions to his plane where the pilot, a tall, slender man in his twenties greeted us, looking more like a bus driver than a jet pilot. His youth would have made me nervous at any other time, but now, as if the gods are beholden to the Sheik's great wealth, I felt wrapped in protection from plane crashes, earthquakes, and floods.

The pilot helped us board the plane. To my surprise, except for a smiling flight attendant, the cabin was empty.

"Are there more passengers coming?" James asked the pilot.

"No, sir," he said.

The plane was furnished like a beautiful living room with easy chairs, lamps, end-tables, the windows were draped in fabrics that were more like clouds than cloths. After taking off, the flight attendant served us cocktails and canapes, a lunch of salmon in a caper and mushroom sauce on gold-trimmed plates, accompanied by a glass—or more—of Burgundy. Dessert was some delicious chocolate pastry that I was a little too drunk to name—not only from the alcohol—from living the luxury of royalty. From having a whole jet plane to ourselves. From exquisite food and service.

Two hours later, on TWA, we were stuffed into narrow seats with our knees halfway up to our chins. When I asked for a pillow and was ignored in my misery by the flight attendants, we were given a lunch of an undefinable sandwich, salty chips, and an orange that had seen better days. Oh, and a wrapped-up cookie. Income inequality now had graphic meaning to me.

It wasn't always yachts and jets. On a trip to Venezuela something I ate made me violently ill. At dinner in a restaurant when I didn't return to the table James sent the waitress into the ladies room who found me curled up on the floor. He got me to the hotel's doctor which, it turned out, was no better than the ladies room floor. The doctor couldn't speak English, and I couldn't speak Spanish, and that's about all I remember of being sicker than I'd ever believed possible.

Another time in Venezuela James had invited two couples for dinner at a restaurant. We knew they dined late, say 8:30 or so, but they didn't show up until 10, and after waiting and waiting and running out of things to say, the only civilized recourse seemed to be the emptying of a bottle of a very nice merlot. So, when they finally arrived I was feeling really, really great. The buzz lasted all through dinner and later at one of the couple's houses where I remember dancing with our host, a head shorter than me, to Latin music having the time of my life.

9

You Can Live with a Broken Heart

I lost my two adult sons within a few years of each other. The fact that I am vague about the exact years of their deaths is one of the strange ways I live with my losses. Another way is to cry only at traffic lights, in my driveway, and in the shower.

Eric had lived with kidney disease for years without telling me, until it worsened to the point that he had to endure regular dialysis. Still, he was able to have a life of work, family and friends, along with his quick wit, opinions on everything, and a loving heart.

That is, until a doctor with a knife killed him.

Trying to remove the scar tissue from his intestine caused by the dialysis, he cut into his intestine, filling him with the infection that overwhelmed antibiotic drugs and his body's immune system. It is of no comfort to know that a Johns Hopkins study estimated that more than 250,000 Americans die each year from medical errors.

Eric was smart and politically as far left as you can get. He was also a feminist; when his first daughter was born, he engaged a female physician as a role model for his months old daughter.

He was an artist with a camera—more artist than business man. If he had not been born in Shaker Heights with its culture of privilege, he would have lived an artist's life, making do with whatever money his art would bring, rewarded by the expression of his creative soul. But he wanted to marry, he wanted a family, and his role models were not artists but prosperous business men. So he went to work for his father in his heating and air-conditioning business..

Eric's breakfast tray lay uneaten, cold and curdled; the toast dried, the coffee, black ink. Because he loved Chinese food I had gone to the restaurant down the street from the hospital and brought him a feast of Chinese delicacies. Smiling—he was smiling! —he watched me open the white cartons with the wire handles and arrange them on his tray. He picked up the chopsticks, put them down, and leaned back on his pillows with his eyes closed.

"Can't," he said. "Sorry."

The nurses had a Chinese feast.

Eric rejected traditional religions; Steve sent his sons to Sunday School and was as far to the right as Eric was to the left. Even their relationship with their difficult father was different; Steve was a cool negotiator, Eric a hot fighter.

Opposite in life and together in death? Oh, how I wish I believed that.

In teaching hospitals like Mass General in Boston, the medical teams change every four to seven days, and I had not yet met Eric's new attending physician. I approached the nurses' station. An aid was focusing on a computer. I waited. I cleared my throat. Finally she looked up. She had brown eyes and long eyelashes. She said the doctor was on his way. She said she heard they almost lost Eric at Baystate Hospital. She said Eric was a sweetheart.

A doctor wearing his stethoscope as proudly as a woman in a diamond necklace stepped off the elevator. He looked important and a little smug walking briskly, imperiously, toward me. He took my outstretched hand. "Mrs. Hughes? I'm Eric's attending."

I looked at the name on his badge. Jeffrey Goldstein. He's Jewish! And from Mass General's Harvard! A great sign. But he doesn't look Jewish. Maybe he has a gentile mother. He had light-colored eyes and blondish hair. And he was young. Who wants a young half Jewish doctor for her beloved? I wanted a doctor who knew about suffering from anti-Semitism. Or whose parents were concentration camp survivors. Or who has a child as sick as mine. A sick child would really be great.

"How do you do," I said calmly, politely. I hoped my glasses hid my black smudged eyes. What kind of mother wears mascara to the hospital?

The doctor's cell phone played a little tune—one of those old-time songs like *Take Me out to the Ballgame*.

He put the phone to his ear and moved away.

I waited.

If Eric dies I will blow up this hospital and everything in it. No, if Eric dies I will sell my house and give the proceeds to this hospital to save the life of some other mother's child. If my son dies I will loathe every mother on earth with healthy children. If Eric dies I will become a nun and devote myself to the leper colony, wherever that is.

Okay, okay, calm down. They're doing everything they can. Think positive. He will recover. Deep breaths! One day at a time. Trust in God, in case he exists. Believe in the wisdom of fortune cookies. Remember to say thank you to the nurses and the friends and relatives who call on your cell phone. Be polite. Do not say that they have no idea what this is like. Do not think how much you hate their stupid clichés. But who knows? Maybe the clichés are true. Maybe that's why they're clichés. J.D. is praying for Eric. So is the man in the super market deli counter and the clerk at the dry cleaners because I explained to each of them that my son was very sick. So if you count all our praying friends, family members, and acquaintances it could very well be twenty people. All praying! More, even, counting the mailman I had also confided in, and the dishwasher repair guy. But God must be busy elsewhere—that is, if God is up there, or somewhere, because my son is getting weaker. Because if half—if one-fourth—of the prayers for Eric reached their destination he would not still be lying helplessly and jaundiced-faced with an uneaten breakfast on his bedside table. I did not pray because I could not bear my rage at its futility. I'd rather accept Sartre's idea of random absurdity than my anger at the indifference of a God who may or may not exist.

I followed the blonde doctor and a flock of interns into Eric's room—the interns like fourth graders on a hospital field trip. But they looked so young and tired I thought crazily that I ought to make them peanut butter and jelly sandwiches on Wonder bread. Playing doctor in their white coats and unlived faces they were trying to learn how to be real doctors. The world was being taken over by kids! We want grownups! This was life and death! Go learn on somebody else's body. Some old person who isn't my son, who doesn't have four young children and a sister and a brother and a wife and a mother. My son has had enough mistakes inflicted on him by the medical profession.

The doctor was speaking to the interns, but I didn't get the words. My sorrow seemed to turn the sounds into some kind of a song. I thought I heard the doctor say, how are you feeling, Eric? But that couldn't be right. What kind of dumb question is that? Is that what they learn in medical school?

"Please wait in the hall. I need to talk to you," the doctor said. I did as I was told. I had to keep the doctor on my side. He has to save Eric. I must motivate him to save Eric. I'll buy him a good dinner with expensive wine. A beautiful silk tie. A cashmere sweater. Blue. Like his eyes. I'll sleep with him.

"Let's go to my office," the doctor said, leaving Eric's room.

"No. Now. Talk to me now."

I thought I saw his eyes moisten. No, I was sure of it. I was surprised. I started to like him. For a crazy moment I felt sorry for this young man forced to deliver bad news to somebody's mother.

"And then there's the polycythemia," he said.

"The poly what?" I asked.

"Polycythemia ruba vera—it's a blood condition that makes too many red blood cells."

"But that's what my mother had!"

He looked interested. "I didn't know it was genetic." It was a cruel, monstrous mistake. I was next in line for my mother's polycythemia. I should have been the one to get it. Nature got its generations screwed up. Nature had gone nuts. It was enough that Eric's kidneys had failed. He didn't need a rare blood disorder that rightfully belonged to me.

"New scar tissue has formed on Eric's intestine," he was saying. "He can't survive another operation, and he can't live with a blocked intestine. We recommend that we stop the dialysis and keep him comfortable with morphine."

I stared at him. Somewhere in a fissure of my mind, or in the pain in my gut, or in my rising stomach, or in the breaking of my heart, or in my suddenly shaking hand, I understood. I got it. They were telling me to let him die.

"I'm so sorry," the doctor mumbled, gazing at his shoes.

I swayed on my feet. He grabbed my arm. "Someone!" he yelled to the group of interns waiting down the hall. Two of them raced over. They half carried me into the waiting room and eased me into a chair.

"I'll call your husband," the doctor said, leaving the room.

My grief was outside of language. I had no words. Well-meaning friends and family found me mute. Dazed and confused at this loss, too intolerable to be real, cannot be real, I was living a continuous tormented dream.

I wanted to see Eric and started down the hall to his room. I heard footsteps behind me and felt someone grab my hand.

"You'd better let me go in there with you," my husband said.

I looked at him. "Why shouldn't I go alone to see Eric" Did James know something I didn't know? Then I remembered. Someone said Eric died.

"I want to go by myself," I said.

He released my hand and I continued down the hall to his room. I had walked this corridor so many times that it had become as routine as all the hotel rooms, rented cars, and airplanes of the last six months traveling from Austin to Boston.

The door was closed, I opened it and went inside. The room was dim. The florescent lights were always left on in the evening until bedtime, but now it was so dark I could hardly make out the motionless figure under the covers in the bed.

"Eric?" I said.

He didn't answer. Of course he didn't answer. He was dead.

I pulled my chair closer. The figure under the covers who used to be Eric was—I remembered the phrase from somewhere—as still as death. I touched his face. It was cold. I sat in the chair because he needed me there watching over him. He was dead. I knew that, of course I knew that, but he was there, under the covers, and I wanted to stay with him.

Jill came into the room. "His wife wants in," she said.

She came over to my chair and put her arm around me. "Please get up. Rosa is waiting." She took my hand.

I let her lead me off the chair because she had offered her kidney to Eric and I loved her for that.

Three years later, Steve followed his brother in death, succumbing to emphysema. He had asthma, and he was a smoker, and it killed him. I didn't know that he smoked until he died because he never smoked in front of me, as if he knew I would try to stop him, save him, yell at him, cry.

I sat with Steve during his last days. I had a book on my

lap that I was afraid to open. I thought he needed my constant vigilance. I thought if I averted my eyes to the book he would die. I knew that was foolish, magical thinking. I knew that, but I wanted to pretend I was keeping him alive because I was his mother and a mother does not let her son die.

He walked around the house with a long wire on his oxygen mask, talked politics as he tried to get me to vote for Bush instead of Clinton in the coming presidential election. A big part of the day was deciding what to order for lunch from the deli. I liked those ordinary, fleeting moments when nothing in the world was as important as deciding between corned beef and pastrami.

Steve's grace, his courage in the face of this terminal illness was humbling and inspiring, and pride and grief nearly did me in. I cannot lose him. My life will turn to nothingness if I lose him. I have known him his entire life. From the moment—the second! —of his life. Losing a child is unacceptable. Because losing a child is like losing your heart. I raised him to be the very nice man he is. I divorced his father which gave him pain, but nothing like the pain I am now getting back. I longed to change places, to take his illness from him for myself. But what chance does magical wishing have against emphysema and cigarettes? Please. Give me a break.

"I hope I make it to the elections," Steve said.

In some kind of cosmic mistake Steve and I had switched roles. The mother is outliving the son. That is not supposed to happen. It's against nature and logic. It leaves an abyss. It leaves a broken heart. It changes everything.

He died the day after we flew home to Texas, as if he didn't want me to see him die.

"We lost Steve," his friend told me on the telephone from Cleveland. I must have cried or something because I was still holding the telephone when James took it from me. I felt his arm around me. I think he led me to a chair—or maybe it was to our bed. He brought me a pill and a glass of water. "To help you sleep," he said. It was eleven o'clock at night on the bedside clock. What had happened to the afternoon? I remembered that dinner was a blur, but little else. James helped me into my nightgown, got in bed next to me, and turned off the light.

I surprised myself by falling asleep. Waking at three o'clock in the morning I thought Steve was in bed with the measles. Measles are dangerous in an adult! Hurrying to his room I remembered that he had measles when he was eight years old and that I dreamed he had died. Standing in confusion, I felt James leading me back to bed.

Language returned to me as mysteriously as it had left, and with it came a need to talk about Eric and Steve: their work, who they were, how they lived—and died—their families of wives and children. So I attempted conversation with relatives and friends. When that didn't work, I tried talking to the plumber who fixed the shower-drain, the cleaning lady, the librarian (who advised me not to look at the past before she turned away). I told the mailman about my sons and that my husband, James, had a job when he was in college delivering mail on the street car.

But people seemed uneasy with my talk, as if the deaths would rub off on them or their children. They changed the subject. In the library I saw Amy Richardson from our monthly canasta game turn away, pretending she didn't see me.

Once in the supermarket I saw Steve's favorite Granny Smith apples and had to leave my half-full shopping cart in tears.

Meanwhile, I had been to three different grief counselors and found each one to be either glib or lacking in substance. Then, by trial and error, recommendations and word-of-mouth, I found myself in the office of a Jungian analyst. After several sessions I felt a connection; she got it. And with her help I saw a path out of numbing grief. She helped me focus as much or more on the good my sons and I had with each other than the losses. She also suggested that I write about my feelings. Although the process brought forth another Niagara of tears, it helped to lift the heavy burden of paralyzing sorrow.

The loss of my beloved sons, Eric and Steve, have, with the help of a Jungian analyst, taught me to focus on the years when they were alive and healthy. Motivated by my pain I learned step-by-slow-step to live with loss and grief. In a culture that denies death, my sons' deaths have shown me how to accept my own death whenever it comes.

So it didn't kill me after all. To my surprise I found myself among the living, doing just about everything I did when Eric and Steve were alive—ordinary, normal, even pleasurable things. I have a feeling of lightness, of being ungrounded without a center as time and psychiatry helped me live with that peculiar inner space where my sons used to be.

10

Living Agelessly

I am often asked how, at the age of ninety-seven, I can still write books, entertain, workout, see friends and family, and maintain a schedule and lifestyle of a much younger woman. They want to know my "secret."

My secret is in plain sight.

Everyone has one.

It's the brain. One of the brain's prefrontal cortex's functions is decision-making, which means that we can use the brain's power to change our negative thinking about aging.

I have the aches and pains that most people my age have.

I wake up anyway.

I work out anyway.

I write every day anyway.

My brain doesn't care how old I am.

The truth is that we can actually change and grow in old age. We have more time, we have more wisdom, we have more experience. I met and married the love of my life in my late 50's and began a writing career at a time when I was supposed to be either dead or in a nursing home.

David Alter, Dr. Doug Green, Henry Emmons, and others have done extensive research on the power of the brain's ability to change behavior. Everything that occurs in the mind creates an effect on the body. If you think your age limits your life, it will; if you think that you can change and grow when you age, you will. But the power to transform your life, whatever your age, begins with making a conscious decision to ignore our culture's negative stereotypes. And not just once—although once is a good start—but often. These are, after all, new ways to think of yourself in the world.

Life comes in a bundle; the good, the bad, the disappointing, even the tragedies are all parts of the whole experience. When we accept the whole bundle we choose life. When we choose life instead of the chair and television, life chooses us. Coping with the challenges, discouragements, and adversity of life is what gives us courage, wisdom, strength and confidence.

Age makes me freer, calmer, less lonely, better friends with myself. I have more of an edge and more softness. My likes and dislikes are crisper. I understand more deeply the people I love. I know the green of spring for the first time, the thoughts in my head, my mistakes. As old as I am, I understand for the first time that each moment is gone forever, never, ever, to return.

What I have learned so far:

❋ Just as your body requires food, your brain needs nourishment. Feed it the intellectual curiosity of beef tenderloin. Pass up the fast food of the superficial and reach past the mind's clutter to its rich substance that can take you to a larger life.

✳ Leave your comfort zone because the comfort zone is reserved for the old. Go forward and take a few risks because if you don't grow, your life narrows and old age beckons.

✳ Believe in the awesome power of the brain (you are ageless) in spite of the culture's cruel stereotypes (you are old you are old). My brain has made it possible for me to publish four novels, a memoir, a book on education and a collection of essays, many in my eighties and nineties.

✳ Aging provides us with time, wisdom, and the kind of freedom that no other phase of life can offer. It is an opportunity to try new ideas and choices, discovering ourselves anew.

✳ Toxic thoughts are poisonous to your potential. The power of the mind is that no thought can be planted without your permission. Therefore your mind is the product of what you have permitted yourself to focus on.

At the age of 89 Doris Haddock began walking the 3,200 miles between Los Angeles and Washington DC, which took her 14 months. Kimani Maruge enrolled in the first grade at 84 years old.

Grandma Moses began painting at 75 and lived to 100, still painting. At 93 Tao Porchon and her 23-year-old dance partner swept ballroom-dancing competitions in New York, New Jersey, and Puerto Rico. A Japanese woman, Mieko Nagaoka, took up swimming at the age of 80 and at 100 became the world's first centenarian to complete a 1,500-meter freestyle swim.

At 103, Hidekichi Miyazaki holds the world record for the 100-metre dash in the 100-104-age category in a respectable 29.83 seconds. Both women are from a culture—Japan—that unlike America, reveres old age.

We are who we believe we are.
✻ Anonymous

Focused mind power is one of the strongest forces on earth.
✻ Mark Victor

There is no limit to the power of the human mind.
✻ Anonymous

The more concentrated it is the more power is brought to bear.
✻ Swami Vivekananda

Ask anyone if they'd like to go back to their youth, and most will emphatically say no—some will actually shudder. And no wonder. It's a time of career worries, relationship worries, money worries, kid worries. A time with no idea of who we are or even what we want in life. And without preparation or support from our culture for the challenges of marriage and child-raising, we feel stressed and maybe even more than a little surprised that these are supposed to be the best years of our lives.

In my early thirties, denying the history of my murdered father and uncle and who I was, I tried to change my identity in the country club life. Since the other women members played golf I took golf lessons. Everyone drank at club parties so I drank martinis. Trying hard to "belong" I entered the club's annual out-door races. But my hands developed huge hives when I took golf lessons, I threw up in the club ladies' room from the martinis, and sprained my ankle in the running contest. It was clear even to me that my body was saying no, this is not who you are or what you want!

We all know that exercise, a healthy diet, and one's genetic inheritance play important roles in our life-span. But perhaps it is less known that our culture sabotages those guidelines by teaching us to fear and despise aging. We are told that when we reach the age of (60—70—80—90…pick your number) we will be relegated to the sidelines of life like a surplus commodity, left to television, boredom, loneliness, and aches and pains. Brainwashed by our culture, we give in and give up on life. It's as if at a certain age we become invisible while youth is everywhere—in television shows, movies, on magazine covers, and advertisements for everything from toilet paper to glorious vacations—not to mention the billion-dollar surgical and cosmetic industry. So we pursue youth with no limit on the money and time and energy we will spend in the search—which is doomed anyway because unless we die, we will get old.

Judith Viorst in her book, *Necessary Losses*, writes, "Within the fear of aging is the fear of death so we look away, we deny its relentlessness and inevitability. But death is so interwoven with life that we close off parts of life when we shun thoughts of death."

She goes on to quote John A Wheeler, "Life without death is meaningless; a picture without a frame."

"If one is not able to die, is he really able to live?" asks the famed theologian Paul Tillich.

Novelist Muriel Spark has one of her characters say, "Without an ever-present sense of death life is insipid. You might as well live on the whites of eggs."

"But age itself can call forth new strengths and new possibilities," Viorst wrote. "There may be more confidence, more freedom, more perspective and more toughness. There may be more candor with others, more self-honesty."

If you think my vibrant life at the age of 97 is because of a charmed background you would be wrong. It is from years of events that ranged from miserable to heartbreaking. It is from looking at the abyss. It is from learning the hard way that coping with the challenges and tragedies and losses in my life are what gave me wisdom and continuous self-discovery.

I have a deep inner peace that sustains and warms me and feels as true and mysterious as a dream.

Maybe it's because of my advanced age, or that I landed on a safe shore. Or maybe it's the knowledge that I have not only survived the difficult years, but against all odds, thrived.

It's been said that all we have in our lives is the moment. The past is over and out of our reach, the future unknown. When we live in the moment, worries about the future and regrets about the past are dispatched, making room in our minds and hearts for agelessness and an authentic life.

So focus on the moment, love the moment, seize the moment. Remember the magic of your brain and bask in the glory of your age.

Other Books by Babette Hughes

FICTION
The Kate Brady Series
The Hat
The Red Scarf
The Necklace

Searching for Vivian

NONFICTION
Lost and Found
The Secret of Happiness
Why College Students Fail (co-author)

CPSIA information can be obtained
at www.ICGtesting.com
Printed in the USA
BVHW030857120220
571345BV00015B/37